Reale degli Antoni

Gigì
An Italian in Nottingham

ISBN : 978-1-911424-68-0
SKU/ID: 9781911424680

All Rights Reserved. No part of this book can be used or reproduced in any manner whatsoever without written permission from the publisher, except in the case of brief quotations embodied in critical articles or reviews.

A catalogue record for this book is available from the British Library.

Editor: Charlotte J. March
Cover and Book design: Wolf

In cover
"Lande Boscose"
by Reale degli Antoni
2016

Publishing Company:
Black Wolf Edition & Publishing Ltd.
www.blackwolfedition.com

Copyright © 2021 by Black Wolf Edition & Publishing Ltd.
and other respective owners identified in this work.
Designs and Patents Act 1988
All rights reserved.
First Edition Hard Cover 2017 - First Edition Paperback 2021

*If only I could grasp your green eyes
with warm stories of Love.
So far away from me...
So far, far away now...*

PART ONE

An Italian in Nottingham

Reale degli Antoni

An Italian in Nottingham

Two years. I had never faced the clouds moving so fast. I had never seen my life changing so quickly. A couple of years that could be the report of an entire life. It's incredible thinking how the plans that I had before had been distorted in such a short period, maybe the most important of my life. Growing? If you don't fly you die here. Changing. This is the first word I need to learn to pronounce next time I'll be born. It was like passing underneath an anvil. I've been eradicated from my land of illusion and now that everything is over, I have nothing but her and a Valley of Stars.

The first person I met getting off the plane was a Greek guy of my age I took the bus with for going to the University. I was very excited because I had been studying modern Greek all the summer on my own, since I thought it would have been a good trick with girls knowing the Greek. Well...to everyone his own illusion. I've always had a passion for Greece and its literature, but in this case, it had to do more with an intellectual issue. A waste of time. I had studied all the summer... and I wasn't even able to introduce myself with him! Since we got off the bus in such a rush and without being sure of our stop, I asked for indications to the first girl passing by. With a lot of embarrassed politeness, this girl of Asian origins took us to the University, which was there, right in front of us. We, the Greek and I, didn't realize it because the concept of campus is something that can't be found in our countries: a city of ideas. Future architects, actors, chemists, politicians, lawyers drawn all together in that place, in a park as big as a city. A real factory of expensive thoughts. There everyone is living an experience that will lead possibly to a job; everyone sporting, getting high, studying, loving in their own way.

Anyway, coming back to us, this Asian girl, as I would have found out within ten minutes, was from Hong-Kong. Bess. At least I hope that was her true name, since Asians usually change their names into Western ones when they come to study in Europe like John or Jack – I've met hundreds of Chinese Jacks – so I'm not even sure that was her actual name. When we put the Greek on the bus leading him where he needed to go, Bess and I finally found us talking alone. It was wonderful because when we were all together, the Greek was ahead with her, complaining about issues dealing with buses and timetables. Even if I was walking behind them, with some curious looks toward me, Bess made me understand that was more interested in me. Yes, yes, I know, I tend to overthink. So when the Greek went away looking for his dormitory, Bess and I felt free to talk and share. She escorted me till the Portland Building, the commercial hub of the entire campus, where she was sure that I would have found assistance for reaching my Hall – truly, I had no idea where to go. As a matter of fact, I always ask myself what would have happened if only I had asked her to hang out.

'If only...' This is my favorite sentence. Many times I watch people in films saying, 'Me? No! I have no regrets!'

Well, my life is a collection of regrets. It was very simple: while we shacked hands, I watched her with a confirming look in my eyes full of future hope, and with doubtful voice I said, 'Well, thank you...Bess?'

'Yes, then goodbye...Reale?'

Both of us uphold with a tiny nod our names that so shyly we declared. I still don't know why, but I was convinced that I would have seen her again. I was almost sure, but I have never met her again. Bess...from Hong-Kong. She was studying medicine and she was doing the second year. She had such a sweet expression, but at the same time, I could see that she felt confident about her successful career and about what she wanted from life. This is all I remember.

I really like girls who know what they want, but there's the risk that they could become obsessed by that. I've always dreamt to be maintained by a business woman or a rich one. I can imagine the situation: I'm smoking a cigar bought with her money, naked on her bed at lunchtime, and instead of finding cooked food on the table, coming back from work she finds this lazy Italian guy smoking, and she's about to kick me off if it wasn't for my charm able to make her change idea. It would go surely in this way! It's strange but I've noticed recently that when I see a beautiful girl fascinating me, her face stays in my memory for few minutes, maybe even for some days, and then disappears. All I'm able to keep are the gestures and the words, like that time I was in Japan, in a school of Chinese people learning Japanese. It's a long story and I will not waste time telling you why I was there, but I think it could be relevant to our conversation if I write about a particular moment. I was sat close to a pretty girl – who didn't speak a word of English. I guess she had a lot of makeup, but I couldn't swear it. Since I didn't have anything with me, she gave me a pen and some paper, without even asking for them. I thanked her and she replied with a tiny gesture with the head. What I'm getting at is that I don't remember her face, except the makeup she had on her eyes, but her kindness is immortal in my heart now. And so for Bess along with all the other girls I'll never see again.

After this hopeful start of my campus life, I headed toward my Hall, which was on the other side of a fucked wide valley. Try to picture me with bags along with the only consciousness of not knowing where to go. I like ignoring the way, but not when I'm pissing myself in the pants! I really needed a toilet. Since I didn't understand what the assistants told me, I gambled and I chose a low path hoping that it would have remained as such, while the bastard decided to betray me and after a couple of minutes it started rising and rising. Because of the rush that I had to settle down, I didn't have the chance to notice the beauty of that place doomed by a valley that will be the witness of many of my most precious memories and that understood me more than many other people. At some point, bam! I spotted a notice, simple and honest, suggesting me the right way. While walking toward my Hall, I saw a very posh place, a gothic house with led and wood engravings developing itself in highness, overhanging an Italian garden on the back.

'We are indeed in the country of Harry Potter,' I thought.

Well, that place that seemed to me very high class style, it was actually the cheapest place of the whole campus, which is another way to say that was my home. In fact my room, shared with an English guy, Steve, six feet tall and 200 pounds heavy, belonged to that wooden house welcoming students on the top while having some working offices on the bottom floor. In general, I liked that house, although it had just three toilets for twelve people. All the other blocks were the same, high and anonymous buildings, while that gothic house was a sort of wooden hidden house on the boarders of the wood, spying young lovers falling in love in the geometrical garden on the West side.

One thing that I've noticed soon in the UK is that people judge less and surely not in such an impolite shameless way as in Italy. Eccentricity – while talking, dressing, dancing – is seen as a positive attitude, something that has to be encouraged. In Italy, for example, long hair are almost banned, and since I was a child, one of the first sentence that people used to tell me was to go to have my hair cut. I had never been able to hold all of this shit. Also the fact that the way of dressing or keeping your hair represents in a sense your political view had always scandalized me. Even the sport is seen as a representation of what you got in your political mind. Why if I have long hair, I need to be seen as an anarchic or teased for being gay – beyond the fact that I've never seen a gay person with long hair. If in Italy girls used to say, 'Well, he's pretty but he has long hair,' in the UK girls said, 'He's pretty and he has long hair.' An English friend of mine once bought a jumper with the image of a Christmas tree on it, connected to an electrical remote system, which allowed to enlighten it. So we used to joke in the dark, turning the tree on and off. Soon after, I've observed with regret, 'Eh... In Italy you could never go out with that thing on. People would laugh at you, considering you a moron, a poor immature idiot.'

'It's a pity,' he said with surprise, 'Italy is such a nice country, but it seems to me that individuality and originality is seen as a bad thing... Also why couldn't I just enjoy and have fun with this staff? Why cannot the others laugh with me instead of laughing at me?'

I should have explained him that Italians have become boring – oh yes the laugh – but for obvious and stupid things. They forgot how to fly.

After all, as you can imagine, the beginning of my campus life was quite hard. I will not tell you the horrors that I've seen while cooking. Difficult was to make people understand me (even if in Italy I thought that my level of English was pretty good, here it was totally different) and impossible was to understand them. I even reached the conclusion that the aim of speaking English is to avoid being understood by the other person you're speaking with. The worst you speak it, the better it is. It wasn't a matter of knowing the language, it had to do more with mental resistance. My lectures were in English of course, I came back home and I had to speak in English with Steve as with everyone else, in the canteen I spoke English, my essays were in English... Well, during the first period I used to sleep in the afternoon from three to four hours, trying to regain some mental strength. The worst was that I was missing my dog and I felt guilty because she had a tumor, and I wasn't with her. I had left her with my parents she had always knew, but not being with her was hurting me so much. I used to dream her dead basically every week and the burden was getting heavier and heavier. She wasn't missing me probably, animals at the end accept things as they are, but I had the necessity to stay close to her and more than once, that Valley of Stars friend of mine was reminding me my dog's nose, wide and dark that thousands of time I kissed. Maybe this is why toward the middle of October I almost decided to go back home and leave the Uni for goods. I had the feeling that I was just wasting my time, while my dog didn't have any. On the other hand, I was thinking that if I had come back home, I would have felt a failure and I would have disappointed everyone. I wasn't among those guys never been away from home, I used to travel alone and to stay on my own since I was a teenager. What would I have done at home? I hadn't established myself yet in the musical environment.

I think the real problem is that I wasn't alone, there were too many people whose ways I couldn't understand. One day – connected to the madness of the first weeks where there are hundreds of absurd events – a race was arranged in the garden of our Hall. I don't remember all the stages, but basically the participants had to run till a point, turn on themselves ten times, eat a pepper – I've seen a girl throwing up – and then put with their mouth a condom on a cucumber, without being allowed to use hands. The guy who won, a tall one studying politics that I knew, was so excited and proud of having won that he was completely out of his mind for the success. He even run for president of my Hall and won.

'This must be the way you gain votes in the UK,' I thought.

I've always wanted to go away from home, but I haven't considered the freezing wind from the North, that rips your soul away and obliges you to hold in your hands a crumb of memories. I felt alone, and that was it. From time to time, it was passing through my mind the tragic thought that with all this money my parents were spending for my education, I could have lived in Thailand for example for ten years at least. Do you really think that in all those years I couldn't have found a job somewhere – even in the musical environment – even without holding a damned degree? I think that I would, and anyway, I would have lived in a beautiful way ten years of my life. Fuck the career and fuck what society imposes you to achieve. Maybe I would have met a pretty Thai girl and settled down over there. However, it didn't go in this way and it was very dangerous thinking about this frustrating things during that period. Especially if I wasn't able to find the sense of staying in Nottingham. Only a few times though I could attend in the night an outstanding and unexpected event: in that cold island, I was inexplicably perceiving a hot wind, probably brought from the Ocean streams, I don't know exactly. I've always loved that wind. Every time I was having a strange thought: I was imagining that that wind had passed through the room of a young couple maybe even in Mexico, in a far and hot country, some day before coming to me, hence I was breathing and touched by the same breeze that reached them as well. After a few months, I've learnt to understand in advance the coming of that warm wind, and so I used to prepare myself to go out, almost as I had a date, enjoying all that humid heat the wind was bringing to comfort me. Usually, it's so cold at night, but that wind didn't care. Even in December, I was able to feel it at least once a week, while English people seemed not to notice it unless I pointed it out. At the end, I had just him to count on to warm my soul a little, although the campus was still remaining very fascinating, since it was created as such. Well, we are talking about the famous English garden, that seems wild but actually it has been subject of an extreme care for details, like the rocks surfacing the creek or the ivy set in the right point. I remember when I was just a child and I went to Ischia, close to Napoli, how my mum loved Sir William Walton's garden. Surely, I was able to find a sort of compensation within the contemplation of nature, also because the only girl who was liking me in the first weeks was a Pakistan girl filling me with cares and attentions: Pammy. There had been many flirts or corrupted sentences that I exchanged with girls, able to cheer me up, but nothing serious. Like the second day a very dirty blond with two blue eyes that would not have gone amiss on a mongoose, looked at me and said, 'Mmm...I like your hair.'

A friend of her took her aside and said, 'What are you doing?'

'What? Come on he's cue...'

And so I told her, 'Mmm...I like your eyes,' but actually all I wanted to tell her when she mentioned my hair was, 'Mmm...and it's not the longest thing that I have."

Maybe it would have worked.

Coming back to Pammy, I've always thought that she had a big ass, although fleshy thighs have always attracted me. At the beginning, I understood that she liked me and it was fine to me till she started having almost an obsession for me, because she loved my music and she thought I was an Italian superstar – poor girl. She started asking me out in a really direct way, asking for a chance.

'Eh...no thank you. I'm fine,' was my prompt response.

She didn't like it at all, she hated being rejected,

but she knew that I have a difficult behavior, allowing herself to forgive me every time. Once Steve went back home for the weekend and Pammy exploited it for knocking at my door while I was trying to sleep. She got in unconcerned about the situation and started to walk around in my bedroom without having any particular aim. I was observing her, laying on my bed, while she was looking at some new scores that I left on my desk. When she went to the window pretending to check the weather, I understood that the only thing she actually wanted was to be kissed, but since I didn't want to create something with her – and surely a kiss would have caused a lot of useless problems – I just turned myself on the other side of the bed, trying to re-gain some sleep. Interesting to notice I had been talking for many months with a friend of mine, Reese, about our female tastes and he kept on telling me how he loved tall blonds with nice bodies. Well, after six months that Pammy was asking me out without success, he started getting interested in her, so that finally she hanged out with someone. When he asked me and to another friend of mine what was our opinion on Pammy, my friend said that she looked quite pretty and that she was a good girl. While I told him, 'I thought you liked fit girls, thin and tall. For fuck sake, she's got a gigantic ass!' Showing the wideness of her ass by opening the arms for matching the size of that horror. He shouted me to shut up, and as far as I know, they are still together.

Reale degli Antoni

Cheese and Wine...a lot of wine

After a couple of weeks from my coming, while I was eating in the canteen with Sam, a long hair guy quite tall who I met the first days of Uni, a girl sat right in front of me. 'So beautiful,' I thought. 'Then why not speaking to her?'

Here, especially in the first weeks, everyone is so anxious to know each others and make parties all together. Let's Rock and Roll! As a good Italian, after twenty minutes of conversation, I asked her if she wanted to listen to my music as excuse for inviting her out, since in my little wooden house there was a small keyboard on which from time to time I used to get tired of inspiration. It didn't seem to me a bad idea. She accepted and she came the same day in the afternoon with a friend of hers and a common friend of ours, Michael, with whom I was studying and confessing my sins throughout that mad year. I played on the piano, I let her listen to some recorded pieces of mine and it seemed to me that her hair like copper with a tiny twist on the eyes level were turning my music in such a superfluous thing, worthy just to be thrown into the toilet. She liked my music however. A lot. The first thing she did getting into my room was to try my big boots that I had brought against the rain. As soon as she put them on, she laughed bending the back together with the knees, since the ocean of my boots was too wide for being filled by her elegant foot and in the meantime, I was wondering why the hell the character of Goethe's *Elective Affinities* drank from his wife's slipper and how he could even get sexually excited. By the way, she was studying literature, but she had never heard of Goethe. Really strange. The fact of having tried my boots and having taken a couple of steps laughing has been a gesture that really took hold on me, since it seemed to me an informal attitude that people have with close friends, not with a total stranger. I remember she told me that she couldn't understand what I was doing there, and that she had always thought when she used to see me getting into the dining room, that my place had to do more with clouds that with a canteen or with the University. Probably she was right... What the hell I was doing there? After all she was a girl able to make poetical comments from time to time, but she was among those confused women living in their own worlds, if you know what I mean. While she was staying in my room, for showing off my artistic importance – such a big mistake – I filled her hands with three acts of a symphonic poem that I had just written, we are talking about hundreds of pages for a total amount of one hour of music. Only when I saw her empty expression watching those sheets meaning nothing for her, I understood that my excitement was due only to a simple fear of being inferior toward her beauty or maybe I just missed the way people acted in the past. Let's face it: I'm too romantic. I made her laugh when I told her a sentence that I said one night when I stepped while I was walking back from my department with a friend of mine. For explaining and justifying my fall, I shouted to my friends, 'I was watching the fucked stars!' I don't know why but she kept on laughing. When the afternoon was over, I took her back to her block and I asked her, 'So what do you think about hanging out together one of these days?'

She watched me with such a sweet expression that made me wanted to kiss her straightforwardly, 'Of course…'

I left her thinking that she was already mine. I was so happy, I couldn't believe it! Later the same day though, I met her again, but she almost pretended as those hours that we spent before didn't even exist. After that day, many others passed through, while she kept on behaving with that sense of detachment toward me. I couldn't understand at all. Have I done something wrong? One night, the Hall arranged a Cheese and Wine – just another way to get drunk – in the library. You can understand now my surprise when she run to me and hugged me as soon as she saw me. Then I've realized. That was my first lesson in the UK: basically almost all English girls are snob or anyway they would never expose their feelings or acting in an instinct way in public when sober – probably because of the Puritans. If they are not drunk, they will never let themselves go, whether they are shy or not. They will always find the excuse of having drunk too much alcohol for justifying their actions the day afterward with friends or with the guy they stayed with the night before (if they still remember of course). 'You must understand me, I was drunk, I didn't know what I was doing.'

This is a very employed sentence. As Italian, I thought that one was supposed to court a girl for getting her. While here, at the end of the world, it doesn't work in this way. You need to go to the same club the girl you like is going to, and try to approach her while both of you are drunk. You don't even need to wait for her to get drunk in the club, since everyone starts drinking before going out, because it's cheaper and alcohol or drugs turn you on already: some of them don't even have enough strength for reaching the club, wasting their £15 ticket. Drunk, in a club, a girl would go basically with everyone, ignoring – or not even remembering – the fact the day afterward. I hate people who try to justify themselves with the excuse of alcohol. If you know that when you drink you'll go mad, don't be surprised if later you've done some bullshit. Don't ask sorry or try to find excuses, you knew it, so just be honest with yourself.

There's a thing, they call it Campus 14, where you got a limit of time for drinking in all the pubs of the campus a pint of beer, meaning that you got to drink in 14 different bars in one single night. A friend of mine once tried to finish the general plan, but he collapsed at the 13th one.

Coming back to us, the Cheese and Wine day I felt as a moron that had just understood how things go here. So I let the copper hair girl be, even if from time to time I still talked to her without though allowing myself to have illusions on her. Once I saw her completely drunk. She run toward me asking me to hug her. When I reached the kiss range and there was only a tiny sky layer between our lips – I will always remember the way she was watching me. She started cherishing my hair, lock by lock, studying my face almost ecstatically and melancholic, as I were a man sentenced to death and she was conscious of being my last earthly experience – it was due to the alcohol, I know. I think she was about to kiss me, but right in that moment, her friends came over, bringing her again that sense of English shame and modesty that you have to keep in public unless you're in a club. She asked me if I wanted to go to a party with her, an event called Safe-Sex, where condoms and strange games were celebrated. I said no, of course, adding though, 'No thank you, but I would like to go in your room with you to have safe-sex together.'

She laughed shameful and scandalized, slapping my shoulder with her nice hand, without using the full harm, moving just the wrist.

Talking about condoms, there's an event I've passed through I thought I had already written about it. Well, when my sexual prospective started to increase – as you'll see later on – I thought I needed to get some condoms at least. Just in case, you know. I heard once a thing called "C-Card" where basically if you obtained it, you could get a lot of condoms for free. The point is that I didn't know how. So I went to the Health Center and they told me that I would have needed to go to see and be interviewed by a doctor who would have been attending a sort of medical event in one of the campus' hall that week. Truly, they arranged this "thing" in the Dining Hall at dinner time, when all the other students were eating. There was a long queue facing this doctor who wasn't holding any event: she was checking and testing the guys against sexual diseases. I didn't know what to do but I queued over anyway, quite embarrassed since there was all the "normal" students eating and watching us. On the other hand though, I felt cool, since only a guy who had an intense sexual life would have done those tests. When my turn arrived, she started giving me all the glasses I should have pissed in and all other things like this, but I told her that I wasn't there for being checked, 'Why you're here then?'

'I just wanted the card to get free condoms!' I shouted full of stress for the whole situation.

She watched me and pointed out to all the other students queuing and told me that there was no time for that. And so I left. The day afterward, I went to the Health Center again, and this time I was quite bellicose. With a very hard tone I told the assistant that I needed condoms and I had already tried to see the doctor standing in a Dining Hall for almost one hour for nothing. A bit embarrassed, she lead me to another doctor who wasn't supposed to work that day. When I saw her, I said, 'I need the card to get free condoms.'

With a very English politeness and attitude she said, 'Right.' Five minutes later, I had my card and my dignity back.

Where were we? Oh yes, the copper hair girl left, making strange thoughts on my indecent proposal, walking with her ass tight. I only reflected on the fact that getting laid was what she actually wanted, so why not talking honestly? Later though I understood that even to a horny girl who likes living, you can't talk in this frank way, and this is a world-wide law, not just an English one. Why we cannot never be honest and outspoken? Why we need to entrench us in a hypocritical mud of social rules? The worst is that since I wasn't keen of clubs or discos, I started having the feeling that I wouldn't have concluded anything with girls in the UK. I've never been interested in one-night-stands, and about relationships... Well, I never believed in them unless there was real love. But what is love? People stay together even betraying or imprisoned in fakeness. Talking about parties, I've never felt so lonely except when there's an event where I'm conscious not to have even one single friend. Meeting new people is interesting, but approaching a drunk girl seems to me just a coward act, especially if I'm drunk too and I even have to fuck her. If you're not proud, well then it's fine, but if you want to give a good impression, especially when you don't know that girl, the drunk sex is nonsense. There was a Scot friend of mine who every time before going clubbing used to close himself in the toilet and downed a whole bottle of red wine, watching himself at the mirror. Once I've asked him why he used to do it. He replied me that only in that way, we could see the demon face-to-face.

    I used to talk often with a girl, Rachel, that used to sleep with the same guy only when they were both drunk and high and then, the day after, they used to act as strangers. Toward the ending part of the first term, she was sat close to me and when he came to our table for saying goodbye before the Christmas break, he made jokes and said goodbye to everyone but her. She watched me and said, 'Such an asshole...'

I didn't say anything but I thought that was her fault.

During the second term, toward February, it happened to have an experience with a drunk girl, Sally, who almost threw up on my coversheet. She was a nice looking blond, pretty and smart – at least that's the way I depict her – maybe I idealize her too much, I know. Anyway, I had already noticed Sally the only time of my life I went to a club. As soon as I bought the ticket few days before, I almost had a heart attack, as I had just signed my curse, because I knew it would have been a bad evening. 'Now you can't go back anymore, you stupid moron,' I thought. That was it. I didn't do anything, I danced with no one. I stayed cross-armed for two hours and then I went back home, disappointing all the people I went with, who instead of seeing an Italian getting off with the whole club, they saw just a lonely, boring, and embarrassed twenty years old guy. Ah, it has to be noticed the primordial psychological gesture of Steve who, trying to make me feel more comfortable and accepted, let his powerful harm on my poor shoulder as if I were a child. I appreciated his useless act though, as I hope he valued the tremendous effort of my shoulder that was able to hold the lead tusk of a too grown elephant without getting broken. The only interested and compassionate look of that evening – although I reached this conclusion many and many months later – was Sally's, this girl that I hadn't met before but for a couple of times. She was two meters ahead and kept on turning herself toward me, keeping up the rhythm of the music with her legs. She was turning around, looking at me smiling and lastly going back to the first step. Her smile was just a hint, and I like to think that she was able to understand my feelings, confused and sad. Nevertheless, these are just conclusions that I'm reporting now, after a lot of time. Truly, I've barely noticed her that night, also because I was thinking more of a way for going back home rather than a compassionate look of a girl I didn't even know.

After several months, one night I was in my room with Steve, or better, in our room, since I was sharing it with him, and in the Harry Potter house there was full of excitement for the umpteenth alcoholic night (at least four per week for a total of millions and millions of pounds spent by thousands of students). Steve wasn't going out and everyone else was getting completely smashed. I went out of my room for checking around, and there's a friend of Sally that was usually quite bad looking, she was like a bird coming from the mountains, but an awful one. This time she was dressed half cat half lioness, and she was pretty hot with the ass out, while Sally disguised herself as a minion. She was so funny like that. She was quite drunk too. I met them in the bathroom, and they asked me if I lived there.

They wanted to see my room... OK, no problem. Well, while I let them in, there's Steve on the other side of the room watching a film, not a porno one. As Sally's friend is speaking to him, Sally is speaking to me in Spanish, in French-Italian, and I thank God when finally she re-starts speaking in English because at least I can understand her. She confesses that she drank a little bit, in a sarcastic way obviously. I'm not even touching her and I'm acting shyly because I had never thought she could have liked me. We have talked maybe twice throughout six months. At some point, cowering on the wall, looking me from a span of distance, Sally tells me that I'm an Italian stallion, that she loves me and after having kissed me on the cheek, she fades away with her friend. – Let's keep it between us but I would have fucked them both... Even her friend that night was worth the shot! – Coming back to us, since I thought it would have ended in this way, I took my underwear off and I went to bed turning the light off – as you know I sleep naked. After not even a couple of minutes, I heard knocking at my door but I didn't want to stand up to open the door because I couldn't find my underwear in the dark. Here Sally is coming in again saying – such a shitty excuse – that she couldn't find her mobile phone, and maybe she left it there. At this point, I'm standing sat without leaving the bed, with the coversheet on my cock, and I start talking to her trying to gain time while I'm looking for my underwear, as in films when there's the guy with a hidden knife while the bad one has the gun aiming him, and he's trying to gain time saying some bullshit that allows him to get the hidden weapon out and kill the bad man. Why bad people in films always wait so long for killing the good ones, these are the great questions of life! When Steve goes out of the room looking for bird-face to come and pick Sally up, she jumps basically on me, kissing me, passing to the mouth-to-mouth. Unluckily, I wasn't that comfortable and I hadn't overturn her on the bed with Italian fury because I had to care about not discover me since I was afraid that Sally's friends lead by Steve the fairy-queen, would have come all together as beasts in the room finding us out during our libidinal moment. Even if we didn't live fully that time, it was a pleasurable event indeed. After a couple of minutes she tells me hugging me between her boobs, 'Promise me never cut your hair...Italians with long hair drive me crazy.'

I could see that. With my head between her boobs, I agreed with a good cheer, saying, 'Yes, madam.'

At the end my fears finally revealed been true, because that sentence, Steve's coming made her flee away another time. Even if she wanted me to go with her at the party, I let it be, since I was convinced not to fall again into the not-me area, into the mask, in what the others want me to do. Take this existentialist! Truly I didn't want to exploit the situation too much because she was completely fucked. In fact, I was told that that night Sally didn't even make it to reach the club, but was taken and brought by a couple of friends of hers to her room. I met her again after a couple of days. We talked about formal things, very, too much English. I was telling her that I got drunk the day before because some friends of mine arranged in secret a party for my birthday and although I've always hated parties, it was a pleasurable experience. Then I threw into the speech a 'How are you? Better from last night?' Such a nice goaded! So that I've introduced the argument. Even if we laughed for a while on her wide language knowledge, the kiss topic didn't come out. She didn't say anything and neither did I. Did I become English? The cases are two: she wasn't actually remembering it, an option not to be ignored, or both of us were waiting for the other one to talk about it. Maybe she was just too shy, or she didn't like me truly. I don't know. Since both of us were going to have breakfast, we sat together, but after some minutes I had the impression that she was almost disappointed by the fact that the kiss topic didn't come out. Did I become English?

Perversions and Possessions

It was September. The first time I saw her I thought she was completely crazy. During a windy and freezing day, she was wearing a top showing the lower abdomen, not even if it was an Italian August. After I saw many girls going out in this way or with wet hair in December after the shower – tales of another world – I wasn't even that surprised anymore. I'd met her few times in a couple of days because we were hanging out with the same corrupted and lazy people. We started talking one night because she was drinking a rum with a pirate face on the bottle, and so I exploited that image for talking about my experience as ship's boy when I was 18. She liked listening to me sharing my life, but I guess that she wasn't believing in everything I was saying. Sally (not the previous Sally, this is another one) was a girl who truly liked to go hard and talking frankly. She liked living by heart, as a sort of free spirit, although her conception of freedom was different from mine. She believed to be able to forget a difficult family situation through drinking, strangling life with life itself as poison and antidote. What I knew though was that I could have never been freed from myself, and that was all. Her dark hair was moved, almost curly, her compacted and tonic body was basically perfect. Sally used to be proud of her abdomen, keeping on showing it to everyone. When I first met her, she was hanging out with a gay guy, as a couple of friends snogging together – I don't think they were getting laid. She liked showing off her strength, lifting him up, as he was her bride. By the way she lifted me as well more than once. I'm not saying that she was a Canadian lumber with bovine shoulders, but although quite thin, she was given an outstanding physical strength. I was even jealous of him, who could stay close to her and keep her in his arms. I envied him so much. That night anyway, she asked me how many girls I had snogged with so far. I told her that I had a date three days before but when I saw her better, I beat it jumping out of the bathroom window. Actually, I had met this girl some night before, and I hadn't spotted her obscene teeth because of the dark. I only noticed her nice body and her OK looking, so when we finally met the day afterward in an enlighten place, I couldn't believe that she was so awful and so I run and jumped through the window of the toilet without even thinking of it that much, since she was coming from a different Hall and with the help of God I wouldn't have met her again. When Sally heard my story, she told me that she couldn't believe that such a handsome guy hadn't kissed anyone yet. She had already snogged with four guys in a week and half, without considering that she could have kissed also girls enlarging the list since that night she didn't tell me she was bisexual. After having spent some hours drinking in the common room of the wooden house, the keyboard room which became by now a lair for desperate people, we went to a famous bar of the campus completely unknown to me of course.

I remember the cold of that walk, and I liked finding consolation in the warm bodies of Sally and a friend of hers whose beauties I was showing off alternating my grip. While I was walking a bit tipsy on a road I didn't know – later that year I found out that this was the shortest way for reaching my department, rather than going up and down and that damned hill! – I remember a gigantic tree, maybe a willow, that seemed to me grasping within his branches the tiny light of a street lamp almost abandoned. I thought it was beautiful. I was even jealous because that tree kept on staying in the valley of the stars, and was enjoying the Moon before me and even longer. I was sad but I was respecting him, considering him as a true friend sharing the same doom of mine. I saluted him with an imperceptible hint of the eyes, wishing him a good evening. I was wondering his opinion on Sally.

At the bar we started talking about issues bound to sexuality and dirty stories of course, and that's why I was able to find out that Sally was bi. I went among some trees down the pub, pissing with Dan, a common friend of ours always drunk and stoned, unable to open completely the eyes. A damned black cat that we misunderstood for a panther freaked us out while pissing, since we thought we would have been dead and fucked. You have a lot of strange thoughts when drunk… Dan was a close friend of Sally, they really liked each others although at that time, she was still considering him as a friend. They were really similar on many aspects, like drinking, getting high, ignoring all problems, and most of all they were studying the same subject, biology. I loved talking with Dan especially the first period of our acquaintance. I always felt understood since he was a guy that even without opening completely the eyes, was able to listen without judging problems and stories. We used to laugh all the time and he was a fucked pleasant guy. On the way back, when I burped merciless of sounds and pollution, he said, 'Oh, you're disgusting,' and soon after that adjective, he threw up almost on my boots.

When we were finally back with the others, Sally told me her perversion. She said that she was dreaming about getting her fingers into my mouth... I gazed a little bit thinking on it as if I didn't listen to what I had actually heard. Then, without even giving me one second more, she took me and put her five fingers into my mouth; I almost threw up. She said, 'It sucks...'

I shouted her that truly she was the one who put her hand into my mouth, and that's why I was the one who was supposed to say 'It sucks!' She started laughing and then she put her fingers in my mouth again. This time though I was more prepared, and rather than succumbing, I bite her fingers and I took her down with me underneath the bench. Basically we jumped on each others and soon after we checked us out giggling. I liked her ways and her perversions...especially her shameless way she was playing out. I had never met a girl who wanted to put her fingers in my mouth in front of everyone. Many similar nights passed by, full of perversions and wild pisses. I remember one day in particular, when I was eating lonely in the Dining Room and she sat next to me ignoring her friends on the other side of the canteen. I made her noticing it saying, 'Why are you not eating with the others? I'm just a shipwreck of solitude here.'

'I don't care about eating with others,' she told me with a very simple tone, 'I want to eat with you now.'

Now. This term was probably Sally's favorite one. She was living the present in the best way for her. In the way she thought to have fun. An attitude totally unknown to me. Not because I'm Italian so to speak, because I met in Nottingham many Italians who liked to go clubbing and knocking themselves out. Truly though, I couldn't let myself share that kind of life, although I would have paid for being one of them. Like Sally...like everyone else I met. I had to realize though, that I couldn't be like them, even if I tried.

One October evening, Sally and I were coming back from the usual perverted night. We walked arm in arm till her dormitory. There was such a deep chemistry between us in that period in general, but more specifically that night that we couldn't help to kiss each others. In front of the block's door, we were looking each others really closely: I started cherishing her hair, and she started doing the same with mine. She used to love my long hair, a thing completely new for a guy coming from Italy. I didn't even realize what was happening.

Naturally I didn't make myself illusions and I perfectly knew that that kiss didn't count much for her. I was already grown and knew how things were going on over here. Anyway, that kiss was followed by a period – around four days – of detachment between us. At lunch, the day afterward, I was curious to see her first reaction: she laughed embarrassed as soon as she saw me. When she came eating next to me, I told her, 'How are you? Did you sleep well? You know why? Because I dreamt that I was kissing you.'

Laughing, she came up with the usual sentence, 'I was drunk.'

Without being surprised, I finished my lunch pretending I didn't hear anything. Even while playing pull for example – she was so sexy with that confident behavior! – she was barely watching me throughout those days and always on a defensive position, almost disclaiming me. Later, I was told from Dan that she was considering me awkward and unsociable, a sentence that I would have always, always remembered, whose perfection and logic. I used to exploit throughout those years when meeting girls or if there was a party and people asked me why I wasn't going.

'Why are you not coming with us?'
'Because I'm awkward and unsociable.'
'Why do you have such a sad face?'
'Because I'm awkward and unsociable.'

It was a very handy sentence to me, for justifying my absence of happiness while ignoring the campus' life. It was a sentence that I would have used to remind myself and other people who I truly was, for avoiding falling into the "not-me" zone.

And then, that night came over. Just like a love

film. I was watching myself at the mirror. I didn't like myself like this. I couldn't accept that the only positive thing of that period, my alchemy with Sally was lost. I was about to go to bed already when I still remember to have opened the wardrobe and got dressed again. I said, 'No, that's not the way I want to live. I'm going out looking for her.'

I didn't know where to start nor if I would have found her, but I was sure that I wanted to show her that I was alive and that I wanted to live! I thought that maybe she could have been in the usual bar where we used to go since it was almost midnight and the bar of the Hall was closed. When I started walking with this idea in my mind, I soon got surprised to see that Sally was simply smoking outside her block with a girl friend of her, bare feet, with a tiny little dress reaching barely her thighs. She spotted me and for the first time during those days she didn't laugh. She was quite serious. She watched me and asked me to stay. When she finished her cigarette, she invited me to follow her to her room. I was staying on the door, crossed arms, while she and her friend were talking. Then at some point, her friend went away, leaving me alone with Sally. I didn't know that it would have been better not to go out that night. As soon as I closed the door saying goodbye to her friend, I got an erection and I thought, 'At least you don't betray me.'

She was washing her face in the bathroom, unconscious that I had prepared what I usually call "the long-speech": a monologue that I offer case by case to girls when the situation is complicated, where I analyze problems, find solutions, pros and cons, if you can understand. That time, I had prepared a nice one.

'Sally, I'm perfectly conscious that that kiss for you counted nothing, especially because you were drunk. But this doesn't mean that we can't have fun as in the past and see what happens. It could happen again, as it could happen that you might discover to feel something for me. Of course, we live totally different lives, but this doesn't mean that we cannot experience each others. I would let you live your life, then when you go back from clubbing and such I could be there waiting for you...'

Well, the long speech didn't stop here but truly I don't remember it all and also, the long speech has always been useless anyway. She sat on the bed while I was still on the door. She asked me to join her on the bed, so that when I sat, I started the long-speech:

'Sally, I'm perfectly conscious that that kiss for you counted nothing, especially because you were drunk. But..." as soon as I finished this sentence, she shook her head slowly, and shyly she claimed, 'No, well...it's not true...'

I stopped myself, I watched her, I observed the green floor thinking about my long speech, reaching the conclusion that it was completely useless and untimely. I watched her again and I finally hugged her jumping on her gently as it was the most natural thing I could have ever done, as those lips have always belonged to me. As we had been staying together already for ten years. Afterward, I left the room pretending to leave a rose on her bed, since she always told me that I resembled d'Artagnan from *The Man in the Iron Mask*, and I wanted to imitate him. Before leaving I kissed that non-existing rose, and I put it with cautious sweetness on her bed. She laughed. She was always laughing. That was the symbol of our love: a never-rose.

Reale degli Antoni

The anvil

'Ah, such a nice day. I really want to start this beautiful day in the best way.'

My mum had just sent me a pack of Italian sweets, there were few but enough for been shared with Sally before the Saturday brunch. During the weekends there's the brunch at 11.30, so that they can avoid giving you breakfast. It was a problem for me because I used to wake up quite early and I got ages before eating. That weekend I was lucky though, having those sweets and a girl to share with. I always knew that Sally used to wake up late, so I had been waiting till 11.00 before going to her. I knocked.

'Who is it?' with the tone of someone just woken up.

'It's me.'

I waited some minutes and finally she opened the door. I was embarrassed because it seemed to me as I wasn't a welcomed guest, because I had just woken her up, because she hated people who get up early and also because I started having a strange feeling. So for defusing, I told her laughing, 'Oh, you're so beautiful in the morning when you've just woken up,' opening the arms, as someone introducing a show, or as in this case...a tragedy which turned later into a comedy.

'Oh...sure, sure,' behaving in a sarcastic way.

'I brought you some sweets...'

'Ah, thank you, but I don't want them. Why don't

you sit down?'

I sat, but I wasn't realizing what was happening, on the contrary, I suppose that you've already understood. I watched her as someone waiting for the verdict from the jury. Finally, she did it. She destroyed me. She put an end to my childhood, to my illusions. She put me on the anvil after having warmed me and hammered so strongly creating a shape changing so extreme which couldn't be fixed anymore by the blacksmith. To those people meeting me after that day I used to remember that what they were observing in me wasn't my real behavior toward life, but just what life instilled in me. I wasn't the same anymore, the dreamer, the poet, the moron. I turned. Totally. And nothing could be done. Nothing.

'I don't think it has been a good idea. We hang out with the same band of friends and I don't want problems between you and me. You...' here her words were strangled by tears. I had never seen girls crying for me. I'd never been cause of any female tear, or maybe yes but I had never seen it from live. In a sense that weep – years later I can say that it was just a show for looking sad and stormed – gave me a sort of compensation, balancing my great disappointment. I was even about to say sorry for have made her cry. Without looking at me, she tried to carry on with her speech – long-speech? – getting the voice's timbre higher and higher and I still don't know how the hell I understood what she was saying. 'You're so sweet and I don't want to hurt you. At the beginning I thought it would have been a good idea but then I've realized that is wrong.'

And here I understood that trying to possess a girl like Sally had been madness, but in a sense, it makes me laugh a girl who's destroying me for not hurting me. It's a paradoxical concept quite funny, isn't it? She asked me, 'Can you understand me?'

I hinted a 'Yes...'

'Are you all right?'

I breathed really slowly, as someone about to sneeze, 'Eh... No.'

I had no idea of what to do. I told her that I wouldn't have hanged out anymore with our common friends, since I wasn't able to make this sort of compromises and I didn't want to see her as a friend. I didn't give a shit of meeting her if I couldn't have her. She even dared asking me if I wanted a hug, not even if I were a child! I confessed her that if I hugged her, I would have kissed her, so I rejected her fucked hug and I welcomed this beautiful day. Such a nice day. While I was shooting the door, I don't know why, I really don't know why, I saw that she had hanged on the wall a sort of steal gobbler which reminded me of a shanty I knew where they called that kind of thing in a particular way. I said while I was already closing the door, 'I like that bumper...'

'What?'

'I like that bumper over there.'

'Ah, yes...' surprised but not even too much. I closed the door. The door on my past. Closed.

I came back home as someone who doesn't want to

live. Steve of course cheered me up. He made me feel understood. Without even looking at me after what I told him about what had just happened, he kept on repeating the magical English sentence, 'You'll be fine, you'll be fine.'

I was there, about to cry, shouting, 'Why for God sake I thought I could have ever stayed with Sally? Why I'm such a moron?'

And he goes with, 'You'll be fine, you'll be fine.'

I was telling him that I didn't want to live anymore. And he was saying, 'You'll be fine, you'll be fine.'

I asked him if anything of similar had ever happened to him. He told me, 'Afterward, I had been fine, I had been fine.'

Well, let's face it, I couldn't hold that rigmarole anymore and so I went out for a walk. I met a Chinese who could barely speak English, but although we couldn't understand each others really well, I had always liked to chat with him even if he couldn't get a word of what I was saying. I liked talking avoiding formality with confused and lost Asians. There were also those ones who tried to get integrated and even succeeded, while others found themselves only disappointed. In general though, as everyone knows, Chinese people stay among them, and surely they kept this attitude even here in Nottingham. When I met him I really needed to get things out of the chest, so I told him everything. After a while, he started realizing the essential concept: Sally broke up with me. Well, it's not actually true because we had never stayed together in a true relationship.

However, he could understand the general lines of what happened, and put his arm on my shoulder trying to hearten me. I kept on talking, expressing my reasons, Sally's reasons, perfectly knowing that he wouldn't have understood what I was telling him, but he wasn't pointing it out after all, rather, he was truly sorry for me. That gesture, that Steve did, few weeks before, that gesture that I had defined as simpleton psychology, that gesture in that moment, done by that person who wasn't getting anything of what I was saying but nonetheless could understand my inner feelings, that act became immortal to me.

I went for a walk on my own and I was trying to sing, trying to ignore my situation. In the evening though, things got worse. They arranged a party for Halloween in that damned little room of my dormitory. I was surprised of how much here people were into the Halloween thing, since in Italy few people celebrate it. Everyone knows that is a quite commercial holiday, but tell me please which one is not. Naturally, I didn't want to attend it. I didn't eat anything nor I wanted to see someone. I was just coming back from the walk when I saw Sally that with her face painted and a bottle of rum was taking part to the party. I was incredulous and I realized once again that everything happened between us before was worthy a penny. I went away looking for a place where to die in peace, till I saw the copper hair girl waiting outside her block. She was drunk of course, and since by that time I had already learnt the English manners, I approached her. She had a red dress, a really nice one, with quite sexy shoes fitting with the dress. She wanted to give me five, but I dodged it, provoking her on purpose. This shocked her probably, and she told me, 'Oh, when will you give it to me?' obviously with other ideas in mind.

I kissed her hand demanding forgiveness. I really wanted to fuck her that night. I don't know why though, she was still coy toward me... Probably she didn't like me at all. She started going on the steps trying to reach her room and so I asked her what she was doing. She used my sentence against me, as a sort of protection, saying, 'I was watching the fucked stars...' and faded away behind a screen of frustrations, leaving me to my illusions and delusions, maybe even too many that night.

I didn't have desire to live anymore. I felt the cheeks completely numb, I only felt as they were falling down on the floor. So I went to the canteen and I nicked a knife. I went to my room – Steve was out – and I tried to cut the veins of my left hand. I've always thought that if I had committed suicide I would have surely gone for the veins-cutting. But there was no cutting! That damned knife wasn't sharp enough! I couldn't even scratch my skin so keen on life. Then I took the keys of my room, they were quite serrated. I started pushing, moving them with strength on my skin, but rather than cutting, I was stripping my wrist. Lastly, I let it be and I shouted fuck off to everyone. I had not been able to commit suicide in the way I wanted. I had not been capable to be loved. I had not been cool enough for getting integrated with the drinking culture. I was only a mediocre inept. The worst of that night was that I couldn't even feel physical pain. While I was stripping my skin with those keys hoping to bleed to death, I wasn't feeling anything – how could I ever thought to commit suicide with keys I still don't know. I had such a strong pain inside me that I knew it could have never been able to match the physical sensations. I really didn't give a shit anymore of living. Nothing. I would have never thought to react in this way for a girl that, especially if I think about it now, wasn't worth my life, wasn't worth anything. Maybe I wouldn't have committed suicide actually. I just wanted to do something. Something that would have hurt. Maybe I wanted me to hurt myself for once, without letting other people do it.

To make matters worse, we, Dan and I, used to have breakfast together every morning. Every day after that suicide attempt, I asked him to tell me in details the events and everything happened to Sally the night before, being scared that soon or after Dan would have got laid with her, since they were really symbiotic. By the way, while talking, I found out that Sally didn't tell him anything about me and about that night. Did I become her secret? However one day, quite shyly, Dan made me understand with a look that something happened between them while I was about to express my usual morning question. Suddenly I thought the worst, but he "hearten" me, saying that they restricted their passion to four players – making even impressions, probably for helping me to understand more. He told me also they were so drunk and high that he was even surprised to have remembered it. I went pale since right in that moment Sally came and took him for going to lectures together as nothing happened. As they were just acquaintances. When they were out of the site, I waited for a while, I stood up and went out of the Hall getting my T-shirt off, groping in the emptiness with my naked chest out. It was almost December.

I was still in love with her after all. Everyday I used to put in practice my strategies for re-conquering her once again, those ones planned in the long evening meditations, finding out every time their ruinous nature. Nonetheless, I had a great idea in my mind, and I had planned something going beyond desperation, a sadist masochist act re-taking in a sense the idea of the non-rose which marked our best night. I knew that she would have come back home toward the second week of December, and so I went to steal a rose from a garden in the campus and made my move before it would have been too late. I went and knock at her door after half an hour shitting myself at the toilet. I hid the rose behind my back, with the stem – whose thorns I had removed before – shoved into my pants. I was told the night before that she got kissed with Dan in a club again, I had realized that our love was impossible, there was no hope to make her understand what I was actually feeling for her, but all these details didn't stop me and my madness. I walked those damned steps another time, the last time, also because I hadn't realized till that moment that I was a complete moron.

'Who's there?'

'Sally?'

She opened the door in a doubtful way, and I was, slobbering in an incessant babble, trying to make her understand that I was there for telling her goodbye before the Christmas break. Then I did it. I gave her that damned rose taking it out of my ass, saying, 'Well, I didn't want to come over here without having nothing for you, and I really wanted to give you something before you'd left.'

She blushed. I don't think though due to any emotion that my act stimulated in her, she had too much of a killer for perceiving feelings, even if that day she maybe had pitied me. Rather, I truly think she blushed for having received a rose without knowing why. With no reason. In fact, this is what her look was telling me. 'Oh...is very sweet from you,' typical English sentence, and I had enough of these kind of sentences.

For avoiding an embarrassing silence, I made her laugh fabricating the bullshit that I broke into a private garden for getting the rose and run away with the flower in my hand while an old woman got me. She laughed, adding, 'I don't want you to steal roses for me.' At that time I would have confessed her that I would have nicked hundreds of roses for her, but if I think about it now...Yes Sally, you were right, you didn't deserve any rose.

I went away and my hands were empty once again. I smiled when I heard her locking the door. Was it all in vain then? Didn't she understand that from the time of our kiss throughout those two months, I was in love with her? So my acts and everything I told her, love confidences, everything happened between us, nothing made her realize my inner feelings? No, she knew. She perfectly knew that I fell in love with her and this is why she stopped our relationship. She was scared of possession. Maybe she wasn't in love with me or anyway she didn't think we could have had a future together, and this was sad to me. Very sad.

That night she really gave me a beautiful good-bye present. Something I really needed for cheering myself up during that period. I was going back to my wooden house, when by hearing some screams and shouts, I already understood from a distance that an umpteenth party was arranged in that damned room with that cursed keyboard. I didn't realize though that Sally was behind me while I was walking. When I spotted her, we made the walk together and I escorted her inside the house. Dan was coming toward us, I had no time. I told her breathless, 'I'll miss you during the Christmas break,' and since I didn't understand if she heard me or not, I proclaimed it once again, getting the tone louder. I don't know why, but she laughed a little bit hysterically and confined. Dan came over and after have told me, 'Hi,' they went drinking with the others. A couple of hours later, I got out of my room for a walk. I had renounced sleeping long ago. On the toilet way, I met Dan. He didn't have any fault of Sally's behavior, and so there was no need to get pissed off with him. He has always been a funny guy after all. We were talking and laughing as usual, when she came over hunted almost by a jealousy crisis, and pinched him repeatedly in the hip, for attracting his attention and playing around with him away from me. Inciting him while talking with me was such a puerile gesture, just like stupid children. So he stopped our conversation – just what Sally wanted from him – turned and started playing around with her running up and down the house. That was the last time I ever felt something for Sally, since I lost any attraction for a person who revealed herself not just as impolite, but as a cruel one, especially in that situation. She took away one of the few friends I still had for jealousy, without granting me not even some laughing moments. Strangely, her unkindness and her egocentrism, her lack of sensitivity, hurt me deeper than I had expected. It didn't actually hit me, it just helped me to be free from that obsession, achieving a sort of detachment toward her.

 I went back to sleep, and probably it would have been better to have never woken up again.

Reale degli Antoni

My murdered friend

When I came back home for Christmas I couldn't even say a word to my parents who looked like total strangers to me. Nonetheless, the food was good and finally I could see again my dog. I used to spend a lot of time on my bed thinking about those months of madness, remembering Sally under the rain, with the hands in the pockets, laughing watching me with a satisfied attitude, as it was her to have caused rain. I started being so scared, so fearful that once back to Nottingham, I could have fallen in love with her again. I was wondering what I would have done seeing her again. Actually though, when I went back to England my fears were completely groundless. Once again I had idealized her too much since as soon as I saw her after the Christmas break, I realized that I wasn't feeling anything anymore for her, or maybe I had just learnt to control my feelings.

Falling in love became too risky for me. It would have been stupid loving someone who couldn't correspond my passion, and strangely, I had understood it. My mind was stronger, and I felt happy and free again – so to say. I started again flirting randomly with girls, although I was still considering myself a shipwreck. I was always eating alone, in a corner away from everyone, even if after a while, some friends of mine that I used to hang out with in the first term – not the corrupted ones – started to join me for dinner. I was surprised. When things go badly, I perform a kind of test. If I pass through a difficult period, a make impossible for people I know to date me, changing extremely ways and attitudes so that they won't stay with me anymore. I do it on purpose to check who's really a friend and who's not, since only a true friend would be able to overpass this wall of appearance. Although I still had some friends, life wasn't that much attractive to me.

To make things worse, at the end of the academic year, I found out that the tree, a true friend of mine I hunted stars with, has been cut. That dragon, ruling the valley along with few other colossuses, wasn't there anymore. His corpse laying on the ground was the only thing spared of his greatness. Talking with those people who cut it, they told me that his roots had a disease, and so they had to. It was so sad. That friend of mine has been killed after hundreds of years of kingdom. I couldn't believe it. I swore on his dead body that I would have taken care of his corpse and memory, and that I would have gone to visit him the more I could, because he was so lonely and forgotten by everyone. Maybe I wasn't doing it for him, was it for myself? Maybe I was that cut tree. Or maybe I was just feeling compassion for a dead creature – because trees are living creatures – whose pride had been destroyed along with his body. I could see clearly his decadence, which had nothing to do with his corporeal fall. His spirit had been banished. He was towering on the whole valley, now he was but a hindrance of branches and twigs. Be free to think what you want to think. I loved him. Although more than once I have seen the sun set, sat on his majestic figure, keeping him company while talking with him about my life, my visits weren't making me feel better at all. I started to perceive his depression, as an old general who had been put in the hospital after having won the war. Where was the glamor of his dark branches? Where was his power? Where was his witness? He was the only one who saw my face, before and after Sally-the-anvil. He saw me the first time we went drinking together. He watched my solitude when at night I used to try grasping wondering clouds in the Valley of the Stars, hoping they would have taken me away. He wrote poems on my love for those warm Mexican breezes. He had seen everything happened to me, and his dead now was terrifying me: he was representing the only witness of my past life, of my changing, and now that he was dead and gone, there was no one spared to know who I truly was.

One day I saw a man carving sculptures in him and modelling his big shapes. I started walking toward him quickly. My confidence was copulating with my anger. It was May. I asked him what he was doing. He told me that he had the permission to make a sculpture in it, and truly, he was turning the tree in a big bench.

'I want to make a place where students can come here and fuck,' he told me.

I warned him to treat him nicely, because the tree was a true friend of mine. As soon as he heard this, he looked at me, and after having smiled with a comprehensive looking, without any sarcasm or any teasing tone, he asked me the tree's name. My protecting behavior toward the tree, faded away along with my challenging tone. I felt as I could trust him. I knew he would have understood. He didn't laugh. He didn't try to change topic or teasing me as those people of my department who kept on laughing while I was telling them about the whispers of the light in the Valley of the Stars. It's a matter of understanding the topic just like that, at a glance, because you know what I'm talking about.

'He never asked me my name, so I never asked his. I think he would get bored of having a formal conversation on our names,' I said watching tenderly his dead body, smiling as someone remembering a past love.

After that sentence, the sculptor and I started having a chat on everything: our conversation dealt with art, countries, moons, sun settings, and girls of course. He told me that I should take it more easily, being more detached toward love issues and taking the positive things life offers us. Well, I thought it would have been easy for him, but for me, it was totally impossible. I strongly believed in Greek pessimism and in Buddhist suffering conception. I left only some hours later, after a long discussion. I felt a bit of sadness in my heart, since watching the tree carved and dig, modeled and changed, hurt me. It made me understand though the shallowness of the shape, pushing me to go beyond the form and to embrace all beings spirituality. I couldn't forget though a great injustice that people made to my friend. As far as his corpse was left natural and rough, no one sat on it or stay there looking at it or even noticed it. The tree was just a hitch for them. Then, when his dead body had been cleaned and his true being was taken away and conformed to the system, his wild ambiguity stripped away, then of course, students, old people, children, started all to interact with him, with what remained of him, with what they could recognize and appreciate of him, a social product, a bench. A big bench. Everyone suddenly jumping and playing on him, not even if it were a playground. Although at the beginning I was angry for the lack of respect that they had for him, afterward I started being happier for I could see he wasn't lonely anymore. Love stories interweaving among his arms, children saying 'Hi' to parents from his highness, and fake intellectuals going getting high on him.

One night I realized or he made me understand a very important thought, a thing that destroyed my Ego and my arrogance that I showed staying close to him after his dead: my true friend has never been alone. He could have helped also my presence, and I even think that my company inspired him pity he couldn't suffer, since not even once, throughout all those centuries, he had ever been alone in that Valley of Stars. When I realized it, I laughed at myself, teasing myself for the importance that I thought to have for him. I begged him to forgive me and my presumption and that night we both raced for seeing who would have kissed the Moon.

Reale degli Antoni

PART TWO

Gigi

Reale degli Antoni

A good academic start

During summer I happened to stay in Rome for a couple of days, dining with some millionaires who had a beautiful apartment on three floors with an outstanding view on *Piazza di Spagna*. They invited me because they liked my music and wanted me to meet up with other artists they knew. I really liked conversing with Antonio – the rich guy – who I started calling "Uncle Toni". He always had a smile, as he didn't have anything to be worried about. He used to talk softly with a very relaxed although confident tone. We were going back from the concert we assisted together, and we would have dined in his house. That night there were also two French ladies – a daughter with her mum who was a successful harpist, with whom I've already spent the whole morning and two Spanish women, one of them in particular was a violinist over forty years old. The harpist's daughter was around thirty, she was a lawyer and quite sexy. In the morning, while hanging out with the harpist and her daughter, I kept on trying to impress them and show off talking about new commissions I received, trying to take hold on the sexy French lady, also because I wanted to fulfill my dream to settle down with a well-off girl over thirty, since she was by then a successful business girl who earned in a month what I couldn't even earn in eight. The anvil-experience of the previous year taught me to chat a girl up without any expectation. Do what you want without despairing if things go wrongly, avoiding idealizing people and living the present without being concerned about "possession". I kept on trying to seduce this French girl all the morning, but she didn't show me her true mind. She wasn't funny, nor that much interesting. She was making me listen to the works of a friend of hers who wrote classical music as well, asking me my opinion and since I esteemed her mother, I couldn't judge too badly the mediocre musical tastes of the daughter, so I kept on smiling the more I could glissando on her questions. At dinner, I started getting on quite well with the Spanish violinist, who seemed to me nothing but a cliché of her country, as her way of talking, her culture, and her horny accent were suggesting me. While I was holding a calix of champagne, she told me that she was guest of Toni and his wife, and that they gave her a room for the night on the third floor of that outstanding apartment still hunting my dreams. However, although I understood that she liked me, I didn't care that much since I was still focusing on the French one, till my hopes turned into a feeling of redrafting when during the dinner, Toni invited her again, asking her to come along the day afterward for joining them for a dinner where there would have been many single successful guys, so that she could have avoided the pressure of her mother who kept on stressing her to get married. I felt the pinch and I fucked the Spanish violinist. Take that!

'Fuck you,' I thought to myself. 'Why do I have to stay here wasting time with someone who doesn't give a shit of me?' Probably I've never been between her charms, and even if she might have spent some thought on me in that sense throughout that beautiful day, by accepting that invite for dinner she made me understand my stupidity. Luckily though, I didn't make myself any illusion, since she wasn't even a fascinating girl. She represented to me just an idea I was fond of: be a kept man. And so, after that moment, I asked the Spanish woman to show me her bedroom, planning to fulfill my revenge. When I got in the room, she watched me with a distorted smile, looking me between light and dark.

'What are you thinking at?'

'I had a strange thought in my mind... I was thinking to kiss you,' I told her with a detached tone.

'Well, maybe you should do it and see what happens...'

I went closer, she was still, looking at me in the darkness of that night soothed slightly only by the shining lamps of the city touching us passing through an enormous window of the room. I kissed her and I took her down on the bed within one second and half. I started quoting her some Spanish poets I knew, while her body was becoming a field of flowers where I could lay down for once. As soon as I stopped acting her the Catalan poems I knew, she begged me to keep on doing it because she was getting very excited. Although she was over forty, I loved her shapely, tonic and wise body, hoping that I wouldn't have run out of poems before having consummated our nightly lust. I asked her if she had condoms, and she, almost laughing, told me, 'Don't worry, I won't get pregnant.'

Probably she was divorced but I'm not sure. Then she took off my clip for the hair, complaining on the fact that since I wasn't gay, I shouldn't have used those female things – her Spanish friend thought I was gay. People are strange: some girls told me more than once during an erotic occasion that loose hair were gay style, while others proclaimed that using elastics for binding long hair, that was actually gay style. I've never cared too much about their thoughts, since one way or another, I would have fucked them anyway, whether I was defined gay or not. While I was with the Spanish, I was getting excited thinking that there were people upstairs talking about boring bullshits. At some point, the Spanish woman shouted for the orgasm so much that I really thought she was about to die, not even if she were a soprano rather than a violinist. After a couple of rounds, we put our minds at ease, and she made me a couple of experienced blowjobs. I was so proud of having chosen a mature woman, because I remember how much girls of my age were posh and acted in a sophisticated way, and few of them would have used their mouth more than once the first night in Italy. In fact, after some months from that experience, I was talking about sex during a camping night close to Milan. A girl was talking about her boyfriend, and said, 'Marco? Eh, he has been waiting long time before getting head.' While she was focusing on her "pureness", I was laughing to myself, thinking that I would have never chosen anymore a girl of my age for getting laid – especially an Italian one.

The point is that after our passion, I realized that no one was still upstairs talking and drinking, except obviously Toni and his wife preparing to sleep. Since I came over with the French ones, I wouldn't have found a lift for my hostel anymore – whose name I wasn't even remembering – at 2 am, in a city unknown to me. Luckily, the Spanish lady invited me to stay over till the day afterward since I took the place of her ex-husband who was supposed to come over that night, and thank God he didn't show up. The last thing I needed was a fight between lovers for writing a Latin novel. The only problem was to have Toni's permission to stay. She put on my shirt and went to look for him. She found him almost immediately and I could hear the conversation, 'Can he stay with me tonight?'

'Yes, but keep the volume down…' probably that scream didn't pass over ignored.

'Ah, thank you…also you know, I didn't imagine it would have happened…'

Even if it was dark, I could see the hilarious expression of Toni, as that sentence was an insult to his intelligence, and said, while he was already going away, 'Oh, come on, we could all see that it would have ended up like this.'

Although all of us went to bed, I couldn't sleep. I had a lot of thoughts in my mind. After a while, I felt a hand on my cock. Offhand, I couldn't understand if she was just resting her hand on my body or if she wanted more. So I pumped blood, moving it, to see what she would have done with it, a sort of smoke signal. She corresponded my gesture, and touched it again and again, till I realized that those two previous rounds were just an entrée, since we started doing it again for long time, although I started getting distracted. A strange feeling started occurring in my heart, as I wasn't caring anymore about what I was doing. I was looking out of the window, while the forty years old woman was enjoying my youthfulness. Then I understood that the excitement was over, and by then I was still giving myself in a generous way only because I didn't know what to do better, since I couldn't sleep. When I woke up in the morning, she was watching me already long before, contemplating my young face that probably appeared to her almost as a "pure angel face", although my shadow looking has nothing to do with angels. I felt my cock so destroyed that I couldn't even piss. There were few words between us. I told her though that her friend, the one who thought I was gay, could have joined us another time when she wanted, since it seemed to me to have proved I had strength enough for both of them. The idea of becoming a two women lover was exciting me so much, for it was a total possible thing, not just a dream. I started even thinking about living with her in Spain or in Rome, as a love-slave, maintained by cherishes and presents. A kiss and I left, looking for my hostel for getting my few things and heading for Nottingham, for the new academic year.

    I used to think about that night quite often. I wanted to prove the French girl that I wasn't caring about her choices, and I didn't need her kisses, since I wasn't a loser easy to be controlled as she might have thought. Rather, I would have paid for having her crossed that room while I was getting laid. The sad point though was that my "revenge" wouldn't even have touched her. I didn't fuck the Spanish only for revenge though, I did it just because it was the only thing I could have done, although it can be said that I was deluded, thinking I could have hurt someone who didn't give a shit of me. I knew that the Spanish would have given it to me, since a positive consequence of the anvil was that I achieved consciousness of what I could have obtained. Don't think though about your stupid cliché like, 'Even if it hurt you, it made you grow stronger.' I had a friend who at that time when I knew him was twenty-four – I was twenty-one. One night he was telling me how his father died and the consequences that his death had on him. He started working since he was sixteen, giving his salary to his family, which wasn't well-off at all. He had a younger sister as well. When his father died, he was twenty-two. Beyond the pain of the loss, he confessed to me that it became extremely difficult to make ends meet, also because by that time, he had been jobless for six months and his mother was earning little. When started commenting not particularly on his situation, but on his loss, I ended up saying a stupid sentence that I would have never used throughout my life anymore, 'Well, although you suffered a lot, now you're a man and you're strong.'

He watched me, and took out from the back jeans pocket a packet of cigarettes, saying, 'Can you see that? Well, I've never smoked in all my life. I started smoking when my father died trying to calm myself down, otherwise I got crisis if I start thinking too much about his death and about my condition.'

This is also why when I was in Nottingham, in the campus, I didn't like that much those guys of my department who seemed to me just spoiled people, saying bullshit and caring about useless issues, just like me with my stupid love problems. I knew a lot of this kind of hopeless guys in Italy, and I couldn't ignore them especially when I was in the campus with pounds wasted every fucked day for stupid things, clubbing and shit. Just one thing was unclear to me: that panic he described me. I thought it would have been connected to pain, but it wasn't. I understood it when I lost a person very important for me. My desperation wasn't only about pain, but that concept dealing with panic became so familiar to me that I totally understood by then what he meant.

By the time I came back to Nottingham, I wasn't deceiving myself anymore, and this was a positive thing because I avoided suffering, but similarly I wasn't dreaming anymore, and this was boring. Life had lost attraction. After all, when I got back to the University I was so full of pride for my Roman experience – or better, a Spanish one – that I felt extremely confident. An experience worthy a lot more than the other love adventures I had that summer. Coming back, I was happy to see again the Valley of the Stars and the tree, whose grave I greeted with a kiss. I was teasing myself for having gone mad for Sally, and swore that I would have never been involved so much anymore. If only I knew what would have happened afterward...

When I started my lectures again, I found out that all my famous and scabrous sentences of the previous year had been all spread throughout my department and even beyond. For example, my favorite one became a scandal. Basically last year we were told to attend a concert and write a commentary on it. The day afterward we all gather together – all students of my year – with a couple of teachers who asked us our impressions on the concert. Well, I raised my hand and said calmly, as what I was saying was totally normal, 'Well, I think those two girls playing yesterday were a kind of munters.'

As soon as they heard these words, some people laughed loudly astonished, others cried, and others more watched me as an anti-Christ. The lecturer tried to reduce the scandal saying smiling, 'Come on, we're here to comment the music, let's leave these aesthetical tastes for other things.'

Even nowadays English people listening to this tale, they can't believe it. Every time I say it, John asks me to tell it again and again, confessing me laughing that he's so proud of me because probably when I raised my hand, everyone was expecting from me a very original and wise comment, while it ended up in that way.

When I reached the same Hall beyond the valley,

I got inside my new block – they had turned the whole wooden Harry Potter house in working offices. I met a guy who told me that he would have come to call me for dinner. When I heard knocking and I opened the door – I was waiting just that guy – I faced six people at least, watching me with a hallucinated look. Many months later, John and Freddy told me that it was the lyrical and cinematographic way I opened the door, shaking wildly my hair, that astonished them. John was a tall guy, even taller of the tallest guys I got used to the previous year. He wasn't big as Steve of course. He was long-limbed and thin, just like Freddy, the other guy I became close friend of. John had a jaw that I baptized as "lazy" since it tended to reach the speaker in a wondering and relaxed way. I had a lot of different feelings that night during dinner. I categorized – in a wrong way – my new acquaintances on the experiences made the previous year. To me, John was just a shallow young guy, who liked clubbing, while Freddy was a typical English man, formal, kind and boring. How much I had mistaken them that night! Spending time with them, I started understanding how much John was sensitive and interesting, corrupted and molest in a different way though from those corrupted people of last year. We could stay together without any hypocrisy and making such deep conversations to be astonished. On the other hand, Freddy had a very English humor, along with a dark side I haven't noticed the first time I met him, a bit like Dorian Grey.

The same night there was a party – fresher weeks

parties – and a blond girl came to me asking if I would have come as well. I told her obviously what Sally taught me, for keeping things clear right from the start, 'No, because I'm awkward and unsociable.'

Contrary to what I thought, she liked my answer. And so I realized that what had been my weakness – or at least seen as such – could have been turned into my strength, into my peculiar quality, an attitude that could have been considered as courage and arrogance of a confident guy, who wasn't scared to be himself, with such a wide experience of life to be able to face loneliness if he wanted to, affording to shit on an invite coming from a blond, if he wanted to. Another girl, an Asian one, dressed as a nurse came and talked to me, usual questions – where are you coming from, what are you studying. I asked her if she was Chinese. She said no, she was English, even if after a short rest, almost embarrassed by my looking, she confirmed me watching another way that her parents were Chinese. I've never understood these kind of racial issues. She had been trying to get integrated for weeks within that drinking culture, but, as well as me, she didn't succeed at all, and basically no one gave a shit of her. I was probably the only one of the block who kept on saying 'Hi,' to her after the first weeks. Just after several months, she started hanging out with a couple of guys – awful ones – that looked like rats. I used to consider what she could think of us, of me, of people more or less socially accepted, ignoring that I had been lonely for most of my life. She knew that she was staying with a couple of losers and she was even proud of them, since I could see clearly that she hated the shame and the fakeness that most people were showing in the campus. I was happy that she was out of it. I could understand her, also because I had stayed with Chinese bands that weren't considered cool guys within the drinking culture and I did it on purpose for putting a seal between me and the UK.

Soon, life brought me John and Freddy to become real friends. We had the chance to test our bonds when a girl friend of John, who was living outside the campus, invited us for a drink in her apartment. The only problem is that she wasn't alone; on the couch close to the bed there were three blonds, heavenly fucked beautiful visions. The point is that they didn't even talk to us the whole night, while the room was getting smaller and smaller. While John was talking to his friend, Freddy and I, standing on the opposite sides of the couch, used to look each others without talking, rather, those blonds even started to practice their German in order to exclude us completely, their sloppy and primary German! When that tragic night was over, we could have said to have become friends after only three days from our first meet. I was extremely happy because I started realizing that that year was going to be totally better than the previous one. I could finally talk with someone on themes – girls, coituses, philosophy, sex, bad jokes – which till that moment had been forbidden to me. No one wanted to talk about those things, making me feel as a sort of outcast. We – John, Freddy and

I – weren't talking about these things for feeling cool or because we didn't know anything else; we were studying these phenomena, considering them as extremely interesting for understanding life and humans. We weren't just young people saying bullshits. We were scientists analyzing and testing our different reactions toward life. Maybe the previous year I had met only one type of English, which had nothing to do with this new generation. They used to condemn me for my honesty and frankness, while John and Freddy used to be fed by my ways – especially with women, so strange in that island, and yet so interesting.

After another damned Cheese and Wine, the three of us passed through a beautiful October evening, belonging more to the dreamy realm rather than to reality, also because we were drunk a bit. We went to the common room of the Hall which was completely deserted, where the ping-pong and the pull tables were overhang by an endless number of sweets, cakes, drinks – probably food spared from a previous party, but don't get deceived if I defined them as leftovers, since ten people wouldn't have been able to finish them all. It seemed to me to stay in a Toyland. Each of us sat on a different couch, and we started talking about philosophical systems linked to Greek tragedies. Within five minutes, three girls we had met the week before joined us for the evening. The nice thing was that each of them liked one of us, so there were three girls for three guys. Truly though, the lucky one was Freddy, because he was the only one who liked his girl – Sandra – while John and

I weren't that much attracted by our ladies, although they were still quite desirable. The point is that Freddy wanted to get with Sandra, but he was also the most drunk of us, and so it was quite funny to see how he strove trying to kiss her, finding however every time the sweet skin of the ladder sofa rather than Sandra's lips, who had nothing but moving herself of a couple of inches for making poor Freddy lose the balance. It took ages for him every time after the failure to recover himself and re-start his battle from the beginning. The girl staying with me on the sofa, Rebecca, would have reminded me later of Pammy, for the stubbornness of feelings toward me. Rebecca had a very sweet attitude, a gentle soul, but her body didn't inspire me sex at all, and actually I've found out that "gentle soul" could become obscure and vindictive. Her voice was melodic, but too weak for my taste. I started acting a bit in a silly way, and after I took a piece of cake and offered it around, I started asking seriously, 'Do you want to make an orgy all together?'

Girls laughed and Freddy fell down another time. So I've tried with, 'Do you want to have a shower just you girls with me alone?'

They laughed another time without any answer. At the end, I had but to renounce to my perversions and quietened myself with my lady, full of frustration.

John and I, sat respectively on the sofas facing each others from a two meters of distance, kept on exchanging glances on the fact that although we didn't like truly our girls, no one could have ever taken an erotic evening away from us. The problem was that John and I kept on spending entire days talking about love, confessing our common doubts toward human relationships. Those glances then were referring to precise dialogues we had throughout those first weeks of our friendship. Essentially, we couldn't fake to like a girl just for getting laid and we weren't even that much interested in one-night-stands. Well, actually he was. He was longing for the principles of honesty and frankness we were declaiming during our sessions, but he never put them in practice. 'Good for him,' I used to think when he was telling me a new experience he just had, because acting only when you feel true things for a girl had been quite ruinous in my life. He had a lot of a club-player in appearance. John was having that kind of life, knowing that it didn't give him too much satisfaction on a spiritual level – although having your body satisfied it's already a very good thing – confessing though that getting laid randomly made him feel good momentarily, even if most of the times he was drunk and he would have never seen again the girl he slept with. One day, I told him that he didn't have dignity, because of the embarrassing nature of the experiences he did sometimes. His answer was clear and confident, 'I have dignity...I drink coffee.'

Truly, he was frustrated deep in the soul just like me, because he used to fall in love with girls he couldn't have, but at the same time, he was able to keep his body sexually satisfied, an excitement which didn't attract me that much anymore, especially after that Spanish night. I was too rational for being ruled by the events, although my so called common sense was simply destroying my life, turning most of the times in an insane anger. John was a paradoxical guy, driving me crazy. Summarizing my studies on him, we could reach the conclusion that John was a sensitive guy who, although living as a player, was aiming to pure Love. Your turn now to get something out of this conclusion!

So our glances, I was saying, while Freddy was falling down another time without success, were much more than just looks between drunk guys touching innocently harmless girls. We looked each others as saying, 'If you kiss her, I kiss her. But if we kiss them, we betray what we said and mostly important, we know perfectly that it's not going to bring us any joy but it will complicate our life and nothing more.'

I was doubting about everything that night. It didn't even seem real to me. Sweets were on tables, but no one ordered them. Each of us had a girl and a sofa, who without having even looked for them, they cowered on us finding sweet cherishes. The common room, which usually was full of people, was totally empty. There were just us with our lust made up of intellectual tones. That one was a fairytale, rather than an alcoholic evening, and I had learnt long ago to doubt about those damned tales. I had a lot of concerns, everything seemed to me too perfect. Hunted by my intellectual winking, I laid down on Rebecca's ties, letting her cherish my face and my hair, trying to soothe all my pains felt till that moment, trying to forget reality. Who cared if that evening was too perfect?! Who cared if it was just illusion?! Those cherishes were more useful than hundreds of poems and dialogues. Rebecca started talking about her private life. Usually, I like when people tell me about their personal problems, but in that case I just wanted to tell her to shut up and keep on smoothing my fatigues with her sweet hands. The Hall outcast, Ron, a red hair guy who kept on trying to get inserted in many different bands throughout the whole year with the only success of been banished by everyone, at some point broke through our world of ideas and perfection, making all of us laughing. He came over without having been invited, of course, getting sat on a sofa on his own, without realizing his masochism: he was blowing it completely, obliging himself to face his solitude. He stirred at us for a couple of minutes, and all of us drunk watching him back, keeping firmly our different ladies on our sofas. We were laughing in a devil way, without even hiding it. There was no formality, no politeness, no manner, no bullshit, there were not two ways around it: we didn't want him and we didn't care about saving appearances. That was the proof on how much that fairy tale bewitched us. By then, all we wanted was to keep our tale as it was, as we found it. Luckily, Ron – not the one who kisses Hermione – wasn't a complete fool after all, he had just problems in accepting things as they were, haven't we all? Wasn't I Ron as well, when I didn't realize I was going to crash against rocks named Sally? Maybe I behaved so badly with him that evening because I was looking for a catharsis and all I wanted was to destroy my past. Once, at junior school, I was around 13, some "friends" of mine started hanging out with some pretty girls of another class. They knew I really liked one of them, but of course, I was never invited. One day, they told me before the lectures that the same afternoon they would have gone for a bike ride with them. Although I wasn't invited, I kept on staying at home hoping that maybe they would have come to pick me up as well. I had cleaned and oiled my bicycle for the whole afternoon. At some point my wishes were answered, and they knocked at my door. I run quickly to open and while a "friend" of mine was talking, I could spot those girls hiding embarrassed behind a distant shop. They didn't come to pick me up. He told me, 'Listen, can you make us a favor? One bike got broken. Can you lend us yours?' Smiling, I went to pick my bicycle, trying to keep the pain inside. I went to take it, I gave it to him and closed the door. At least the bike hadn't been oiled for nothing. Coming back to us, Ron went away after a couple of minutes, in the same way he came: alone. His arrival though had a strange effect on us, as remembering the presence of an external world. We went out of our tale, and reached a garden of our Hall. Freddy collapsed on a railing while throwing up. While Freddy was vomiting and John laughing, I heard the sound of the strokes echoing on the Trent river, it was 2 am. Its waters were bringing away all the sexual and alcoholic bigotry, marking with its oily piss the Uni environment. The only important thing is to have a white, a Chinese and a black all sat together on the grass, smiling on books in a picture. That's the way you save your face. Everyone knows what's going on, the quintals of drugs passing in the campus every week, the indecency of the ways, and alcoholism perceived in the air. Nonetheless, many people consider it as nothing but a normal life experience. Wandering around for months on my own in the forest when I was 16, that was a true life experience, not getting high in a club. They put pictures of Gandhi when he came over visiting in the 1930s, but they never expose pictures of fights between drunks or girls fading on their rooms' doors, without even been able to open them. It seems now as if I am Marlon Brandon at the end of *Apocalypse Now* when he goes with: 'We train young men to drop fire on people, but their commanders won't allow them to write "fuck" on their airplanes because it's obscene.' Do you want to come at the end of the river for getting my head now?

Many times I heard the sentence: 'It belongs to the University experience,' which has nothing to do with the idealized version of Harry Potter, here there are no spells for recovering you from the hang-over. Once, a really horny girl two years younger than me, when I was in my third year, invited me to attend an alcoholic evening – like the Campus 14 but in the city center. If I got irritated when a girl invited me in my second year, you can imagine the answer that I gave her in my third one.

'I don't give a shit of getting drunk and maybe getting laid with a random girl,' but actually I wanted to tell her that I wouldn't have got laid with her not even if she made me drink a lot because I've always hated people obtaining what they wanted only through their sex appeal. She was very sexy. Then I added, 'I've already experienced this kind of culture and I run away from it half-burnt after I understood that it wouldn't have led me to anything. Anything!' And she, who used to get higher marks than me, said with arrogance as if she were advocating in front of a jury, 'This belongs to the university experience.'

'This belongs to YOUR university experience!' I thundered shaking the fists and defending hardly all the pain I felt in my first year. Nonetheless, since I'm Italian, considered by the whole department as a narcissist crazy, wise at times, obsessed by sex, she laughed with a friend of hers of my fit of anger, which seemed to me to have made her even hornier since no one probably in the whole UK would have ever answered her in that violent and solemn way. My frankness while talking and my aggressiveness while gesturing, when it wasn't a scandal stoke, I think it inspired sex to English girls, too used to politeness. So, instead of making her understand my position toward the hypocrisy around the campus, it seemed as I was agreeing with her words. She didn't understand me at all! How many people are actually having fun when they go clubbing? How many people are not doing it just for the fear of being different from others or because they are so sexually desperate whose only option is to chat with a girl who's not even able anymore to distinguish the world's colors? And now, with the coming of the technological era, everyone takes pictures of they alcoholic evenings for having a proof that they are actually living those moments, scared of not being able to prove it to the others. And on the contrary, how many people hating clubs end up inevitably in a sort of caste where what is thought to have avoided has truly become a tragic mirror? There was a band of people like this – I used to call them "The losers of the JCR" – always the same every year, arranging Quidditch games with mops between their balls. They were such an obvious cliché: people thinking at themselves as cool ones because they weren't making the life that people like John was doing. They were proud of their thick glasses and of their bodies lacking of any masculine substance. I didn't have anything against them till I found out that they were even more arrogant of those clubbing guys and they represented just another social layer marked by rules, just like in the clubbing environment.

Concluding: there's no way to help it, in a way or in another. It's like the revolutionary guy who after decades of fights, becomes what he swore to battle against. An option that in a sense I had systematized has been to gather all together the international guys of my Hall, with whom I used to spend my time when Freddy and John were going clubbing or staying with people I didn't like. I gathered during the second term two Chinese, a Cyprian, a Pakistan, and another Italian who came over to study in my second year for only five months at my University. I recognized him as Italian as soon as

I saw him putting chocolate cereals on Nutella, without having even the need to check his nationality. The "Internationals" went to constitute a pleasant, faithful and interesting option when I couldn't hold John and Freddy's friends anymore. I wasn't willing to accept two friends if this meant "to get the whole packet" and so I had this idea of going to talk to these strangers, nothing more than social outcasts, becoming slowly their friends. At the end of the day, I could say that they have always attracted me, because I could see in their eyes of recluses a lot of myself. Surely, they haven't been able to get integrated within the University society, a bit like me during my first year, but I could say that I had been a lot luckier. They were guys who didn't stay with anyone, although the Pakistan kept on trying to act as an English. I was astonished of how much they were able to understand me in my essence, perceiving what I had felt throughout those months. Once, during a friendly fight, I shouted in a frustrating way because I hadn't been allowed to smash the head of my enemy, and the Cyprian, from the darkness of his small and carved eyes, watched me and ascertained referring to the power of my inhuman scream, 'This is you.'

Probably their poor level of English didn't help them to get friends, and surely there were no student deputies who could have ever represented them, us, since all those voting shit constituted only a farce for people like us. We didn't care at all about who was winning the elections in our Hall, which was just a trick for making politic students playing among them, making them feel fulfilled with their fried ideas eluding themselves to be able to change the world. One important thing is that the ideas dealing with relationships and love of Alessandro, the other Italian guy, would have been a substantial psychological reef to overpass after the events that would have happened to me toward February.

I'm perfectly conscious that a puritan regime dealing with a kind of "National Prohibition", would turn fakeness into much bigger fakeness. Young people want – and sometimes need – to experience these kind of staff. My concern deals with the attitude the whole University society has in elevating this sort of clubbing life as "the life", the best and most logical option you got for growing, for chatting girls up and for making friends. I don't want things to change – otherwise no one would ever get laid anymore. I'm just condemning the hypocrisy spreading around the University, when high profile people say that they are proud of their students and especially I'm trying to burn down to ashes the irritating illusion of control that parents have, unconscious – or maybe pretending to ignore it – that buying drugs in the campus is literally easier and quicker than getting food. The university as institution of course is not supporting this, but I cannot even say that they admit the actual situation. Once I still remember, I was waiting for a friend of mine on a road close to the Valley of the Stars, and within 15 minutes, I saw 6 drug dealers delivering their staff to single students on booking. Just like if they were selling candies. Surely most of the students are able to get a prestigious and high valued degree. What actually have they learnt though? This is why I've always hated those parents escorting their sons around the University during the open-days, with an accomplished and serious look, as they had any control on their sons' lives, as if going around visiting the university environment during day time with a guide smiling and explaining you everything would let parents getting any idea of the real campus's life. Why don't you invite parents in clubs at late evening? That was just hypocrisy that I wouldn't define as English, but in general, as belonging to the parenthood area. One day father and son came to me asking my opinion on the University, while I was reading in the library. I replied in a frank way, 'Well, if you're ready to pay for the psychologist and the doctor, then I insure you, you'll be fine.'

Kansas City move

While the English sun was warming her image walking slowly on the shores of the lake, she was pretending to be a light wave of fresh water. By her lost and concerned moves, it could be seen that she was asking to the lady of those putrid waters – more suitable for hunting than walking – if it would have been the right thing to do. Would her life have changed? It's curious to think that six months before, I also had walked along those shores, deep in the night, scared but fascinated by the sublime of the forest kissed on the forehead by heaps of stars. It seemed to me to be under the water level and see the world from the abysses of the silent ocean.

By then her relationship was nothing but a social façade exhibited on internet and among friends. The guy she was staying with had become boring and empty of any substance. He had never given her any satisfaction. His marks weren't good at all, he didn't have any ambition and was quite childish. All he longed for was to play Frisbee – a sport that in Italy is restricted to dog's entertainment, while in the UK, as in many parts of the world, is considered surprisingly in a very serious way. Surely, she's a very demanding girl, she knows she's quite beautiful. She wanted to change life, but she never had the chance to test her courage, even if she has never been that intrepid after all and as we all know, it's so difficult to leave the old path for the new one. That day, she questioned the quiet waters of the lake, but as usual, the muddy doom leaves us uncertain, letting us take the hardest choice at the last moment, which is never the right one. It always seems as there's a lot to lose, idealizing the other person only when you got to leave, an attitude belonging to the human fear of loss. She was never able to decide.

I used to question Destiny while wandering through the Valley of the Stars, trying to understand what would have become of me. Obsessed as I am by success, I was doomed by the idea of not being able to see beyond the time I was living, without knowing what luck was planning, also because for me, the present wasn't a gift at all: it was a curse. Yes of course, it was going much better than the previous year, but I was still considering myself as cast in a prison, an academic cage I couldn't run away from. Everyone saying those bullshit like, 'Today is a gift, this is why is called present.' Everyone with their positive attitude and shit. They have never seen in the darkness of a stripped soul who Kafkaesque wonders in the emptiness. It comes to my mind what Rebecca told me once. One day of my second year, we were all in a bar and I couldn't see any way out from my life and I couldn't run out of the window like last time, remember? Truly, the present has long teeth, ready to fuck me over biting my cock as that whore of *Little Red Riding Wood*. Rebecca couldn't stand my sadness in that occasion, since she was very sympathetic toward me as you know. She said, 'You have to be happy.' Those words had no consequence but confirming my thesis: there's no happiness, this is why someone has to impose it on himself, on his exhausted shoulders, just like an evening medicine, more suitable for committing suicide than for soothing pains. I went to sleep that night without thinking about tomorrow. Sleeping was a good medicine to me.

One October night, while I was playing ping-pong along with John and Freddy in the JCR of my Hall, a couple of Chinese guys came in for playing pool. I didn't care of course, although I recognized one of them, really thin, tall at most one meter and half. We say, 'Hi.' Suddenly, bringing table games and different types of Chinese dishes still warm, other Chinese guys and girls were joining them. I've never seen these people before, and actually, I've found out later that they were from another Hall, quite close to mine. Probably, they had all arranged a sort of evening to spend among them. Although focused on the ping-pong ball, my hawk-eye couldn't help to spot a quite pretty Chinese girl playing pool with them. 'Nice ass,' I thought.

I couldn't understand why she felt the need to lean on the pool table, since she was quite tall for an Asian girl, taller than me actually of a couple of inches – I'm not tall, just to give you a term of comparison. I kept on glancing at John, trying to make him notice the presence of that nice girl, and he let the jaw corresponding my luxurious looks, letting it free from the face plant, as he wanted to fill the distance between me and him, standing on the opposite sides of the ping-pong table. I had already known a couple of Chinese girls, but nothing of serious. There has always been in my Hall a Chinese girl dressed like Sailor Moon, with skirts coming from videogames and very high boots. She had a crush on me, but because of her level of English, we couldn't even make an actual conversation. I remember once she made me a compliment for the cape I used to dress for mourning because of the death of the tree, but when I tried to take this chance for having a conversation, we couldn't carry on more than half a minute. She could barely speak English, I didn't know a word of Chinese. Should I have tried with Italian? She made me laugh once, because she gave me the chance to see how the world goes and how the society develops: she had been in the same Hall of mine for two years, but she didn't get it on with no one, not with Chinese, not even with my German friend who dated her. The German even told me that they couldn't carry on their meetings because she didn't want to do it before marriage... Moral Chinese rules similar to ours of two hundred years ago. Then of course, there are different situations where girls don't give a shit of these ethic principles, and fuck a different guy per week and they don't need alcohol for achieving what they want, smashing the European idealizations that conceive Chinese girls as pure and innocents. One day I saw that Sailor Moon's friends introduced her to a Chinese guy – quite awful. They hanged out in the evening and in the morning they presented themselves hand in hand right in front of their friends for breakfast, a clear and agreed social gesture that made friends understand their established union. The girl was so happy, finally she wasn't ashamed anymore for her lack of men, yet, she seemed to be a bit sad. Besides this girl, I had met just another one from China, at the end of my first year. She wasn't that pretty and didn't have a nice skin, although she had an OK body. Nonetheless, I wanted to give it a go because she seemed interesting to me. I chatted her up while we were all queuing over for getting dinner. We started talking about everything, even if I knew that the first time would have been a quite short approach because she would have surely sat with her Chinese friends. I took the dinner slop and I left it on a big table in the middle of the Dining Room, and went fetch some "bread". When I came back I saw a dish in front of mine and I didn't realize whose dish was till she came with a glass for me as well. So we began talking again, about my music, about her career, but soon enough, I had the feeling she was quite boring and I couldn't stand the horror that kept on inspiring me her mouth every time it was swelled like a balloon for eating a whole egg. I don't like conversations when topics don't flow naturally and so after that time, I just let her be, although an English friend of mine told me that it's been long time since Sally-the-anvil that he hadn't seen me talking with a girl in such a calm and serene way. He knew what happened after Sally, he knew the whole story, but he didn't understand what I had become and couldn't get my tireless masochists tastes.

However, the girl playing pool that night looked to

me a lot different from those Chinese girls I had talked to in the past. She wasn't pale – being wan for Chinese is a mark of beauty, not like in Europe – and her face with exotic treats coming more from the Pacific rather than from Asia, her long and dark hair and her size reminded me of the tropical atmosphere of the Mutiny on the Bounty, with my beloved Tarita. Yes, I know, I have a lot of imagination, but I really thought she was Malaysian or even from Hawaii. Just for the thrill of it, and also for showing off in front of my friends, I started walking toward her, without knowing that that decision, taken for stupid reasons, would have changed my life. Actually, I didn't care about it that much because I was focusing on another girl in that period. I used to wait hours for her to pass through, standing on a rotten bench – always fucked wet – close to the Trent building. I had noticed her during a rainy day while she was holding the umbrella with elegance and endless sweetness. When we faced each other and she smiled at me in a honest and clear way, I realized that I could have approached her. I thought her inwardness was quite fascinating, although I didn't know anything about her, and I liked it. I didn't know her name, so I started referring to her during my weekly confessions with John and Freddy as "the mulatta", since the color of her skin wasn't actually coming from the deepness of Africa, rather was clearer. I only knew that she was a very thin black girl with dreadlocks, with a refined and personal dressing style, walking calmly with a reflective behavior. I used to wait for ages on that bones-breaking bench because I saw her passing by the Trent building once – the most prestigious structure in a sense, with its big clock in the middle – but I hadn't met her yet. After one week spent waiting for her – probably I didn't get her right schedules – I ended up thinking that the idea of the bench had been a ruinous one, also because even if I saw her, the problem of how to approach her was a big one. It would have been too *anti-sgamo* – in Italian slang, it refers to a too obvious action that is supposed to be hidden but it's not. One day, while I was walking back from my department, I saw her sat with a guy around the Trent building. I spotted that she pointed at me with the look, as asking him an opinion on my figure. I felt observed, but I thought that it was a positive thing either way, at least she had noticed me. I kept on walking indifferently, confident of my persona, but quite frustrated because I knew that I couldn't approach her: there was that guy and I couldn't interfere. Also… Which kind of relationship there was between them? He could have been her boyfriend after all. When they didn't watch me anymore, I took a way – I knew every corner of the campus – that would have brought me on a higher place allowing me to observe them from the back. One day, from the same upland, I watched the fireworks of a Chinese celebration reflecting on the lake, and I thought that all those colors couldn't match the Moon spying me from the forest. While I was watching "the mulatta" with that guy for understanding their relation, I noticed that he was trying desperately to make a move; he used to stretch the arm trying to hug her for cheering her up or something like this. I guess she was that kind of girl with a lot of personal problems – everyone has issues after all. Maybe she was telling him some of her problems in that moment, and he – something that I usually do as well – was exploiting the situation for creating a physical contact as excuse for hearten her. Although he kept on setting in practice this technique, she wasn't yielding at all, rather, she stayed in a close position, looking down, with crossed arms which, passing over the stomach, were able to land on the ground as dead leaves. She had an absent look, as she was day-dreaming about someone she loved – not me of course. Even if she kept on having this kind of inward attitude toward him, I had to go quickly for avoiding making my jealousy raising up throughout my veins clogged by the rage of not being with her. So that night, my mind was ruled by the idea of "the mulatta", rather than by the figure of this Chinese girl.

'Can you play the piano?' I asked her getting closer to her right shoulder, obliging her to turn toward me.

'No, I was just clicking randomly the keys,' she said laughing.

She offered me the perfect chance for chatting her up, when she went to the keyboard without knowing she would have given me the go for the assault. I hadn't noticed till that moment her nose, so fine and elegant, that was making her different from many Chinese or Malaysian girls, owners of a bulbous nose, reinforcing my suspects on the fact that she was coming more form the Pacific.

'What's your name? And please don't...'

'Jackie.'

As soon as she said that her name was "Jackie", I winced up insulted and begged her for telling me her true name. I hated the idea that a girl so beautiful gave herself such a shitty meaningless name, not female at all, only because of the easiness it could have been pronounced by lazy students, a name having nothing to do with whom she was and with her culture. After I have told her that I was a music student, and that was the main reason why I had been intrigued and approached her at the keyboard, I started having the feeling that the conversation was waning, that her English was pretty poor and that it would have been the end of our acquaintance. As soon as you perceive there's the lack of something, you have to leave before getting embarrassed when you chat a girl up. Surprisingly though, she went to fetch Ma Chang, the most famous Chinese table game, and tried to explain it to me, embarrassed till death by the poorness of her language. I found this a quite brave decision, since carry on the conversation would have been difficult for her, and I think not even her friends expected it.

'So this,' and took a rectangular piece of wood with a Chinese character engraved on it. 'Well, this keep it for later.'

'OK...'

'This...' she took another one. 'Also this one, you keep it for later.'

'Ah OK... I got it...'

'Oh this one! Well...this one is too difficult to explain so I'll tell you later.'

'As you wish.'

Well, after all these slovenly attempts to make me understand the general lines of how to play that game, we moved over a sofa and started talking and sharing. We were laughing, because her name was actually difficult to pronounce; not even when I was one week born I ever tried to emulate those strange sounds. I told her the lie that I not only liked Chinese food, but I used to have it as often as I could. Although the conversation was going all right, I wasn't finding her that much interesting. I thought she was a bit silly and lacking of substance. Nonetheless she was still quite beautiful. The problem was to isolate her from her friends and to find a secluded place, since no one that night would have been able to take a snog away from me.

'You know, there's a nice historical pillar few minutes walk from here. Do you wanna see it?'

'What does "pillar" mean?'

I knew what I could have, and I wasn't interested in talking to her without any other purposes. I didn't have anything to lose.

'You know, there's a nice garden with a river really close to our Hall...'

'I can see you like nature.'

Well, at the fourth attempt I was able to convince her to walk out with me. I just wanted to let myself go for once, beyond illusions. I was so surprised when finally she accepted that I didn't even know what to answer her. I just wanted to feel good and get on with a nice looking girl. I felt quite cool when Rebecca almost drunk came looking for me in the JCR, while the Chinese and I were going down the steps. She shouted me from the stairwell, 'Where are you going? I want to stay with you for a while!'

'Eh, Rebecca, I'm coming back soon don't worry... Ciao.'

And I run away pointing to my lady the quickest away out from Rebecca's jealousy. Later, I've been told that Rebecca was so angry that she got completely smashed that night. I thought that now that the hardest step was made, the game was already won with this Asian. She had expressed quite clearly her interest – although in an indirect way – so it was completely useless to get bored with conversations I didn't give a shit about. While we were walking in the Valley of the Stars, toward the level of my dead friend, I told her getting closer with a fuddy-duddy face, 'What if I kiss you?'

Moving away she said laughing embarrassed, 'Probably you'd be too rush...'

So for avoiding silence, I changed quickly the topic and I started telling her about the fallen tree. As soon as I started talking though, she seemed to me quite saddened from my apparent absence of any feeling. She was suffering probably because of my ataraxy, or maybe she was sorry for having disappointed my hopes because she could notice my incipient detachment toward our acquaintance. In fact, the proudest being of the whole valley, although I kept on talking as I didn't care that much about that rejection, inside me I was writhing. I thought, 'So, I chat you up. You like me because otherwise you wouldn't have kept our conversation alive. I try for two hours to understand what you're trying to tell me, with you bullshits I don't care about. You agree to leave your friends making a public act of going away with me, and then, when I ask you a kiss you reject me? What you got in your mind for God sake?' I felt insulted but I'm not someone who imposes himself, so I put my hands in my pockets and I took her in a garden behind the library. I've always liked that place, so metaphysical, especially when the Mexican wind was visiting me. I was able to stand her bullshits maybe for ten minutes then I took her back to my Hall. She kept on trying to soothe my frustration telling me that it would have been nice to have dinner together and try different Chinese dishes. I didn't care at all about what she was proposing me, and since there was no point to stay there with the consciousness of undertaking the usual social procedure for a damned kiss, I kept on listening to her without adding anything to the speech, telling her simply that I didn't care, while I was regretting to have lost an evening. I was ideally in love with "the mulatta", and I didn't care at all of this girl who wasn't even coming from Hawaii. I just wanted to spend a nice evening snogging and sharing cherishes for a couple of hours. I brought her back to her friends and I said, 'Ciao,' to her without even looking at her. Fuck off.

  The morning afterward I was disappointed, but I

wasn't that much angry anymore with the Chinese girl, because I thought that spending all those months in that madhouse, I totally forgot how the external world goes. Actually in my first year, I realized that it was December only because I saw in a pub the trailer of a film I knew it would have gone out for Christmas and I understood that I wasn't caring about the world from long time. So when I wanted to kiss that Chinese, I completely forgot one has to court a girl. After all, that part of me died underneath the anvil and I decided not to come back. That night, while I was walking around the Hall, I saw again that Chinese girl playing table games close to the JCR. She was basically standing, she was so tall. She saw me. I said 'Hi,' to my Chinese friend, but both for pride and to avoid seeming that kind of guy who haunts a girl, I didn't even say 'Hi,' to her. I just left.

Some days afterward, while I was walking toward the library thinking about all these past events, I saw "the mulatta". 'Finally!' I thought. Since I've noticed she was walking on her own, I run after her because I was determined not to sit down anymore on that damned rotten bench waiting for her. I took the chance, 'Hi, do you mind if we walk together for a while?'

When she smiled at me, I had already understood her answer before she said, 'Yes.'

'I saw you around sometimes, and since you really attracted me, I couldn't hold back from introducing myself.'

We started talking about the usual formal things,

and I understood that I wasn't wrong when I judged her a very idealist girl, with strong principles, involved in political ideas. I talked to her about Herman Hesse to prove that I could top her, but she confessed me that she haven't even finished one of his books because she found his writing style too hard. She told me she was vegetarian, and I shivered thinking if only she invited me for dinner, since I've always been a merciless carnivore. The more I was talking to her, the more I was realizing that I didn't like her so much. I could see a hard girl to cope and to stay with. A girl whose ideas could have been against mine. I always liked being the "acculturated one" in a relationship and I've always hated confrontation. Paradoxically, I prefer a bit silly and non-intellectual girl rather than one who goes protesting publically against the umpteenth injustice. I don't like discussing when I know I'm right, I hate arguing when I know I'm wrong. Among the other things, she told me she really shared my passion for wandering around the woods and that here Nottingham was full of green areas and lakes. Although we kept on talking, it was always me to carry on the conversation and to propose new topics, terrified by silence if ever had happened. She never started the conversation, and I began to feed up with her lack of proactiveness which was clashing with those smiles which pleased me when I didn't know her. When we reached a cross road, I made up an excuse and I pretended that I had to take the other way without asking her for a date. Her name was Ashai.

After one week from that approach, I received the strangest e-mail of all. At the beginning I couldn't understand who had sent it nor how he/she could have obtained my address. I started guessing who had sent it when I read: 'Can you pronounce my name? I hope you practiced,' and so I understood it was the Chinese girl. It was a very childish e-mail, quite *anti-sgamo*. Basically she was asking me if I brought my violin with me in the UK and if I wanted to play for her a melody she really liked, but truly, she was just trying to have an excuse for meeting me again, overpassing the disappointment of that night. Since I got used to the complex mind of English girls, for me it was like a child's play to understand what she really meant with that e-mail. She didn't have any abysses. My first reaction? Anger. That e-mail was just confirming me she liked me, bringing me back to the kiss-moment. Why running away from your feelings? It didn't seem to me she had a guy. And then why rejecting me? Soon after though, I started appreciating her courage and her initiative. I had never met a girl so brave to send an e-mail without any expectations to an almost unknown guy, with the only wish to meet him again. I wrote her in a detached way, sure that soon or later I would have fucked her. It was just a matter of patience. That week my thoughts were still with Ashai. I was thinking whether or not I should have talked to her. I was puzzled by her apparent lack of emotions, except shyness. Maybe I had idealized her too much. I didn't have any idea of what I would have done. Surely, I wouldn't have sat again on that damned bench, by then I had rheumatisms all around my back. The Chinese invited me to a Halloween party, but I refused because I didn't want to re-fall into the not-me, especially for a girl I didn't care much. Moreover, if I didn't come to terms with English girls, surely I wouldn't start now with a Chinese whose culture wasn't marked by clubbing as part of the whole courtship. Now it was me to have the upper hand. I wasn't interested in meeting her, it was her who wrote me so if my ways weren't OK, then ciao, ciao.

One Friday evening finally we arranged a date in the JCR where we first met two weeks before. I didn't have any expectation and surely I wouldn't have got laid, since I knew more or less how things go for Chinese girls. I would have got satisfied if I had snogged with her or had some four-players since she was a nice looking girl. When I saw her I didn't know how to act because I wanted to create this time a physical contact indirectly: I had planned to seduce her. We play ping-pong, while the losers of the JCR are making a sort of Karaoke. For making her laugh, I start teasing our common Chinese friend, playing on my knees for making an impression of his size. Tired of that music, I bring her downstairs and I play for her on a keyboard. I was very curious to know how the hell she had been able to get my e-mail address. Laughing, she confessed me that after our first meeting, she went to the canteen and saw a sheet where I signed for confirming my presence in a ping-pong competition. She knew my name was Reale, and since I was the only Reale on the list, she found my address on the University register of all e-mail addresses of the whole campus. No doubt about it, her enterprise was fascinating me, especially if I considered that she was doing it only to meet me again, something that was making me even angrier because I was thinking that instead of doing that whole annoying process, she could have just kissed me when she had the chance. Take me for example, I've never been so avant-garde like while trying to chase after a girl. If I like a girl, I could be able to wait for her hours and hours in a specific point, but I've never been so smart of conceiving plans as hers. I remember a time when I had a crush for a girl of another high school. I hanged out with her just once and naturally I hadn't asked her for another date. I didn't know how the hell I could have seen her again. She was French by the way. And so, a freezing November morning I had been waiting for her out of her high school: I was relying on the midday break, but she didn't show up. I thought she would have come out for 1.00 pm. Not a sign. Maybe she had gym and was going out at 2.00. Well, I had been waiting till 4.00 pm then I left hopeless when I found out that I had icicles in my hair. I failed to see her, in return, I got a damned flu!

Since I was aiming to seduce her, I was acting with the Chinese in a very mysterious way, telling her about my stormy past and then I asked her if she wanted to walk around the valley with me. She agreed. I brought her back exactly in the same garden of last time, but leading her in a more romantic and niche little place whose way I had studied during the afternoon for avoiding missing up in the darkness. I didn't want to fall into the lake you know. I thought the bench over there was perfect: isolated from the other on an elevated position, was right on the Moon's face reflecting itself into an artificial lake with a little Zen-style island in the middle. While I was leading her over there on a steep path, we took each other's hands as it was the most normal thing in the world. That kind of physical alchemy between us was totally strange to me because I tried the whole evening to clasp her with my right arm while I was making jokes, with no physical answer, bringing me back with the mind to the close attitude Ashai had toward that guy. Her English didn't get better of course within two weeks, and she kept on asking me, 'Why?' of everything I was telling her. It was starting to irritate me: the sooner I would have kissed her, the sooner we would have put aside those social bullshit and spoke clearly. At least, after a kiss, I could have told her to stop with her stupid, 'Why?' It was very windy, and so I gave her my leather jacket for covering herself. She didn't like it but she took it anyway. Asshole. The Moon was full, my lover. Sat on that perfect bench, so suitable for a kiss, I was discussing my intellectual reasons why I didn't appreciate the fireworks for the Chinese celebration happened a couple of days before. With a very baroque gesture, I was pointing her out the Moon.

'You see? The Moon doesn't need to show off. She is just like that. She doesn't need to appear great with rhythmical games and exotic colors. She stays there

and drives me crazy without doing anything in particular, while fireworks are just typical human behavior.'
'Yes, because they are artificial... Artificial?'
'Precisely.'
The strong wind kept on playing around with her hair. The third time her hair had been messed up, I went closer her and fix her dancing long hair behind the ear, while she kept on watching the Moon, almost without caring of what I was doing. I went closer and I kissed her neck, just below the ear, thinking, 'If you reject me also this time, I'll leave and you won't make me come back even if you find out how many times I go pissing.' She watched me as she too wanted to let herself go for once, ignore the context and everything else, and kissed me. I found myself suddenly quite uncomfortable because she wasn't opening the mouth that much, and I couldn't snog as it should. She explained me later that in China people don't open too much the mouth while kissing, and so I had even to tell her how to snog. Surprisingly though, I found myself not that much interested in kissing her, I don't know why, maybe because I wasn't a teenager, and so I couldn't get satisfied just by snogging, also because in the campus, you needed but get drunk and wander around pubs for kissing even ten girls per night. So I let my head lay on her thighs, a lot better than Rebecca's ones. I let her look at me from above, thinking that she had a nice face indeed: geometric but not boring, long-limbed and fascinating. I let her cherishing me as a wild beast longing for a bit of heat. We started talking finally without those stu-

pid social limits imposed by formality and destroyed by carnality. At some point, while talking on how long she would have stayed still in the campus, she suddenly changed position, sat right in front of me, slammed in a very elegant way the hands on her thighs, coordinating the whole process with, 'I don't want to loose you!'

I said so many bullshits to make even Confucius laugh. For bypassing her possess desire, I started being very poetical, getting away with it by exploiting my passion for literacy. I told her this night would have been immortal and we would have remembered it beyond anything which could have happened to us. More or less I was able to daze her with all these empty words, and since I started being cold, I told her, 'Why don't we go to your room in your Hall? But don't worry, not for sex, I just want to stay with you in a warmer and more comfortable place.'

'Ah OK, actually I was already scared to have to tell you how things go in China…'

'No, no, don't worry, I know.'

We left that bench hand-in-hand, and reached her Hall. We went upstairs and got inside her room. After half-an-hour from our coming, we made love several times throughout the charming night.

I've never seen a more beautiful room. Mine, John's or Freddy's were total disaster, in which we lived comfortably. The first day of my second year I had put my mattress on the floor, overturning vertically the steel structure of the bed against the wall. I was sleeping Japanese-like, but in a more corrupted way. I liked laying in that way also because I don't think someone had ever done it in the campus, and I've always been fascinated by new paths. The girl's room on the other hand was totally another thing: there was a double bed, with candid cover sheets and a warm and sweet duvet surrounding the bed, not even if it were a soft snow blanket. Everything was perfectly ordered. Pencil and pens on the desk – I usually stole pens when we needed one, since I kept on losing mine around – candies on shelves – I didn't even know for how long I hadn't touched a jujube – and the floor was totally clean. My room didn't allow you to see the floor anymore, since Babylonians piles of books and scores were on it, and the bed was covering what remained of the floor. I used a jumper as pillow, she had two wide ones, with even a third one which was a big puppy tiger. Enchanted by that portentous dream, I laid down on the bed after having taken my shoes off of course. She sat on an armchair on the boarders of the bed. We were holding each others' hands while talking from the limits of our continents. I could see clearly that she was feeling guilty because both of us wanted to do it, but her moral rules were forbidding it. We were young, alone in a room, but we couldn't do it. I was fine after all even without having sex, since I went out that evening without any expectations. I was holding her hand, cherishing it from the bed, while she was telling me about strange and fascinating places I had never heard. At some point I said, 'Well, we cannot have sex, but there are a lot of things we can do even without doing it actually,' betting on four-players of course.

She jumped on the bed, and I started taking her clothes off. She had a pearly body and a great physique that I didn't dare leaving it exposed not even for a while to the English cold, since before long I let my body on hers as doing snow angels. When I started touching her, I realized the softness of her skin, similar to her gentle floral cheeks. It was like when I used to stand underneath the cheery tree, having my face cherished by the flowers moved by the wind without forgetting to thank them at every gentle touch. It was a precious sweetness indeed. I looked her right in the eyes, and I noticed she had a horny rabbit expression. Accomplice the four-players, she whispered in my ear, 'If you want we can do it...'

'Are you sure?'

'If you want of course...'

At night, I fell asleep having half of her body on mine. I was naked of course. She had a rose and white long dress which opened itself on her thighs: it was beautiful. It was a cloth which was making me idealize even more her Asian lines. It seemed to me like one of those sarongs which had captured Gaugin's soul when he travelled around the tropics looking for peace. I never had problems in falling asleep, and I've always loved sleeping when I'm tired, on the contrary she couldn't sleep at all, and so she went to her desk finished her essays while I was dreaming. At some point she came back from the bathroom, and when shut the door, I woke up. I watched her as I was blaming her. She told me sorry and locked the door. Truly though, I was just dazzled a bit, in my drowsiness. I didn't even understand where I was. I felt guilty for her excuses and fell asleep again.

Reale degli Antoni

Gigì

I wouldn't have seen her again for sure. I didn't want to keep on hanging out with someone who would have gone 5,000 miles away from me within four months. I was longing for easy life. I already had some other girls on the list waiting to be seduced. By then I wasn't interested anymore in meeting Ashai again; she seemed to me too problematic. During those days moreover, I had met an English girl quite nice looking, dark hair with green eyes who from time to time used to play on the keyboard of the JCR, and so one day I took the chance and I went to introduce myself as musician. I owe that keyboard basically every achievement I did, not even if I paid it for being there. As soon as I saw her, I knew she could have liked me, and her apparent shyness was driving me crazy with sexual excitement, almost as inviting me to an assault. By the way, when I first met her, there were also my Italian friends down in Nottingham visiting me. I think she was feeling quite embarrassed and outnumbered since she was alone in a room with four Italians, three of them barely able to speak English. The Ghetto, as we called our group years before, came over many days before I met Ashai or the Chinese girl. They came over before my "love problems" of the second year. I didn't declare to the Hall office their presence in my room, so every day we were quite wary and kept a wide eye when going to have a shower or to piss, since in every block there was a tutor watching over. Tutor Camille's room, with even a personal bathroom, was placed right next to mine, a couple of yards from the block toilet, so we really needed to be quite careful. One evening, the bathroom was occupied and Niccolò really needed to free the fish and chips he had in the morning, so he knocked at the tutor's door shouting, 'Fuck Camille, open this fucked door that I need to shit off!' It was an anarchic behavior learnt after the French Revolution that we used to put in practice with "important" people for challenging the hierarchic social order. After having studied it actually, we started shouting to teachers and even to the headmaster "Resignations or your head" or "Guillotine" during our usual high school lectures. It was quite funny.

We slept all together on sleeping bags they brought and actually I didn't care since I was already on the floor with my Japanese bed since September. It seemed to me to be like *Snow White* dwarfs in a cabin into the woods. When Michele saw my room the first time, he shouted in a rampage of chaotic rage, 'It's a fucked flophouse.'

It seemed to be during the Second World War, and to have hidden Jews in the house, since without showing it, I used to nick extra food for them in the canteen, bringing it to my room for feeding the Ghetto's obscure stimuli. At night we were quite clenched while sleeping, and there was the wardrobe which was annoying Raffaele's head position. I heard something, but then I fell asleep again. The day afterward he told me, 'Well…

that stupid wardrobe was bothering me, so I headed it good night.'

They were four very funny days that cheered me up. They gave me a break from madness. When they left I was sad of course. But actually I felt frustrated when soon after their departure I started with my "love stories", since I wanted them to see those girls I was dealing with. After all there were few simple rules in the Ghetto forged after bad experiences. A couple of years before I was hanging out with Alessia, a dark hair girl I knew since I was 17. It always seemed to me she liked me, but in a sense, although quite pretty – really Italian looking, if you know what I mean – she never interested me that much because at that age I kept on aiming what I couldn't obtain, and so I had never asked to date me. After my first year of University though, I met her in a summer day in my hometown and I felt a moron because I had never dated her when I had the chance. Surprisingly, she asked me to hang out with her that night. I remembered that she was staying with a guy last time I saw her, so one of the first things I asked her during our date was, 'But…your Claudio? Are you still seeing him?'

'No, no…I left him because he started annoying me too much. Eh! I told you remember some years ago? I said that not even if I were a desperate girl I would ever stayed with someone like him. Remember?'

I was so happy, so ready to kiss her as soon as the situation would have allowed it.

'Yes of course I remember… Well now there's Dario.'

I watched her astonished, thinking, 'Why the fuck you asked me out if you got already a boyfriend? Do you think I give a shit to have you as friend? I've got friends already!' The evening was going very nicely, we found out that we had many things in common even on the personal level. She really understood me, and this was a problem: the more the date was going better, the more I was getting angry because there was no point. Whether it would have been a good evening or not, she had already a fiancé, and so that date would have lead me to nothing but sadness. There was a moment, when she confessed to me she considered me a really special person, that I wanted to break the glass and go away. Why? Just tell me why? So from that day, I forged the first rule of the Ghetto: 'Never leave the Ghetto' since outside it, there's just pain.

Coming back to Nottingham issues and to my thoughts about that Chinese girl, I left that room made up of kind snow in the same way I arrived: without expectations. I had spent a nice evening and it would have been enough for me. However, things didn't go in that way.

She started writing me some day afterward, asking me to avoid telling our sex night around my Chinese friends since in China getting laid is seen generally as a really serious act. I calmed her down, but I asked her also if she was regretting it, 'Why? Experience right?'

Those words took hold on me, because I felt completely excluded from her life, from her future – as it was supposed to be – and the fear of separation was torturing me, as I was about to lose a small gem I had just found after many hardships and heart pains. I didn't want to become a little story or a secret she would have told her friends or to her daughter long time after, I wanted to be more. I wanted to be important for a person. While all those thoughts were tearing me, she confessed me to have seen me while I was walking back to my Hall that same day, but because of her shyness, she didn't dare to reach me. All those thoughts which I was wrenching on – whether to see her again and invest in something I would have lost for sure within few months or ignoring her and carry on with my easy life – faded away completely when I wrote her without even minding it if she wanted to see me again or not that night. She told me joking, 'What you want?'

'Come on, I'll be a perfect student and I too have essays to work on. So why don't we stay in your room and study together?'

Five minutes afterward, I was again in that beautiful room, on her bed, studying with a fuddy-duddy face, while she was scanning me smiling from the desk, doubting that I had come only for studying. We started knowing each other better. I've shown her some pictures of me when I was younger, while she was telling me about people she really cares about. She always had relationships since she was 13. I guess she's among those people who can't stand loneliness. While she was talking, I was thinking that I hadn't understood yet if she were a virgin before me or if she had had already sexual experiences. She told me about her last boyfriend, how had been horrible the first time (the only time) with him. She really wanted to forget it. After that day in fact, she had never said anything more about it. I was glad that I wasn't the first, otherwise I guess I should have really got married her. She told me that the only time they did it – once, throughout one year and half of relationship – she didn't feel anything, and so in a sense, we can say that I had been the first. She had already tried to leave him several times, but she felt guilty because when she had been hospitalized for a month, he had been very careful toward her visiting quite often, even doing her homework. I looked at her a bit confused, 'I'm sorry but you're telling me that you had been hospitalized two months ago when you were still in China, and the guy made you all your essays and staff for your love, and you left him soon after? I don't believe you. I think you're still with him, right?'

'Yes...' bowing eyes and head down.

'And you didn't want me to say it to my Chinese friends because you were afraid that they would have told him?'

'Yes...'

It was turning me on. Being the lover of someone – also more than just one – had always taken hold on me in a fascinating way. Burning nights and manly pride. I took the news very well, but I was starting to be jealous. I laid on the bed almost if I were looking the stars sat on the grass of a warm and lonely park. My face was reflective and I had not will for thinking or judging, despite my intricate and paradoxical ethics. Everything had a sense now: she liked me but she controlled herself during the first weeks for she didn't know what to do, she couldn't understand if betraying her boyfriend for me would have been worthy more than just one-night-stand. A relationship? Not even when I kissed her she understood her true feelings for me. Probably the original plan was to sleep with me for having a good reason for leaving her boyfriend, but surely she wouldn't have left him for me. She confessed me that one day of the last week, she had walked slowly courting the shores of the lake close to my University with deep thoughts and doubts and only after that day, she decided to live by heart and to send me that brave e-mail. She understood that this would have been the turning point of her life. She realized that the situation was unsustainable and that it wasn't worthy anymore to pretend liking each other. I told her that at this point she was like a melody of mine to me, and that I wouldn't have let anyone else to play it if unable to read it. I wanted her to leave her boyfriend not for me, but because she was a too good looking girl for staying in the hands of a moron.

'Gigì, is that OK if I call you Gigì? A bit French like...it's nice, isn't it?'

I was smiling while she was describing me the guy she would have liked to get after the Nottingham experience. In particular, I remember her woman wish to find a sexual mature guy, a sentence that reminded me an output that John once told me. I was hanging out with a girl some time before meeting Gigì. We were getting on quite well and she kept on saying that I was the kind of guy she truly wanted, someone really mature. John kept on pressing me for concluding and sleeping with her.

'Yes but what kind of maturity I show her if I fuck her and then I leave her, since I don't think we could stay together in a relationship?'

'Sexual maturity man!' with a very defined hip movement.

By then I was going every night to Gigi's, leaving her room soon in the morning for coming back to real life and to my close Hall. She always woke up late. The problem was that after the first night when we did it, we weren't getting laid anymore because she was afraid that her thing would have become too wide, causing shame and embarrassment when she would have found another guy. She didn't want to seem as a whore. I think she was completely mad making herself these problems. Every night I was sleeping naked of course, while she still had that beautiful Indonesian dress that many times I crossed till unspeakable points, every time stopped by her soft and firm hand. The point is that the lack of sex was a problem. I had to write a couple of musical scores for two different commissions and I had to finish my essays of course and no sex. Absurdly, she wasn't giving anything anymore, rather she was demanding a lot. She was making the error of considering herself the only girl of the campus. For two days she had kept on stressing me for writing at least in part one of her essays. I tried to explain her that I'm not a Chinese, and that I had other things to do.

'But it's a sweet thing you would do for me.'

'Baby, here I'm called Reale the Mean, so since you're good in math, I guess you'll understand.'

One night I couldn't hold it anymore, and after only six days from our first kiss, I made her cry with my verbal power of destroying people. We were on the bed, and she kept on saying, 'No essays no sex.' I had always shown off my freedom, stating that I'm not among those guys who can be enslaved by their girls with the excuse of sex. I changed topic – maybe also for provoking her, and I told her about an erotic dream I had the night before on a quite fit girl of my department, adding that I would have fucked her gladly. She watched me, 'Adieu…Ciao…this is my bed,' pointing the mattress we were comfortably on. Probably, she felt insulted.

She didn't have to repeat it twice, I got up and started getting dressed without even talking. She was still on the bed, with her head between the pillows. When she noticed that I was serious, she jumped on me astride without allowing me to put my shoes on, saying straightway 'No!' as for avoiding the inevitable, 'I thought you were joking. This is why I've been staying on the bed.'

'I'm not joking at all.'

'Come on…I wasn't serious before…'

'To me, you really looked serious and I really hate people excluding others as if they are on the way and unwelcomed. You can keep your fucked mattress. You keep on stressing me for making your essays when you know perfectly that I'm collapsing for everything I have to write and compose. And also I'm not your fucked slave! Have you not any respect for my life? We're not even getting laid anymore and I don't even know why I'm still coming here every night. Nothing but being stressed?'

With a tiny whisper she dared saying, 'I'm sorry.'

'I don't give a shit of your apologies!' I started getting the volume up while was till sat on the bed, with her head down, having me right in front of her, 'People think to be able to justify their actions saying these magic words little words. For me they are just meaningless words! I don't need your apologies and you're making me even angrier! Never ask for sorry!'

At this point I had cut her any possibility for talking. Tears started falling from her sad eyes while she was sprawling on the bed trying to hide it. I was still standing, 'Why are you crying now?'

'Because I feel so miserable when I'm misunderstood. It was just a joke, really.'

'Even if it were, this doesn't justify you for the way you have been toward me in the last days, as in few hours I had become already your slave. I don't belong to anyone. I'm a wolf, you cannot think to treat me like a normal guy. I hope you're not asking me for sorry another time now, are you?'

'Please sit down and calm yourself, then we can talk again.'

I was about to sit down, but then I remembered that there was no time for mercy or sympathy in that cold environment. So, just before putting my ass on her damned chair, I blocked myself and gave her a killing blow, 'Oh, I'm sorry...this is YOUR chair.' And I left. She tried to keep me holding my arm, but I was really too harsh for yielding. I told her on the door, 'If you want, write me an e-mail and then let's see. Don't write apologies. Write me something else.'

I came back home so pissed off that I could have killed someone just for breathing. To make things worse, the next morning I received a pitiful e-mail. She wrote me that she made a lot of physical exercises as every night, and that she was missing the dog of her grandma – I don't like little shaven dogs – and bullshits of that kind, finishing with, 'So I'll wait for you tonight.' I wrote her just one word that made her tremble as she told me later, 'OK...'

Truly, I didn't even want to reply her. I didn't care about her that much anymore. Nonetheless, the sadness of the loss was starting to make its own way through my stubborn heart. It couldn't end in this way. I wouldn't have seen her again and would that be the last memory of us? It was so strange the way things went and I felt almost as if it was meant to meet her that October night while playing ping-pong. If I think about it actually the circumstances were extraordinary: I chose Nottingham among three other universities in the UK. Usually the second year people go and live out of the campus, while since I didn't have good friends in my first year, I had decided to stay in the same Hall. In the meantime, thousands of miles from my plans, a Chinese girl was applying for doing five months in Nottingham, since her marks allowed her to, as opposed to her boyfriend who didn't have good ones. It was to be asked: would she ever let herself go even if her boyfriend would have been in Nottingham as well? I don't think so at all. Everything was happening without our knowledge. One day, no one knows why, that girl who, although living close to my Hall we never met, comes to play pool in the JCR of my Hall the same night I'm playing ping-pong only because there are some friends living there. I think that only a fool would ignore all these events or maybe you're a fool if you start idealizing them, I don't know. What I know though is that I went to her door once again, with a blue bonnet covering part of my face hidden in the darkness of her Hall's yard, and after I pretended to have been forced to enter in her room – I didn't want to be an easy job for her to bring me in her room again – we started talking. No doubt she knew how to get on with me and I couldn't be angry for too long with her. She perfectly understood I just needed a bit of sweetness for calming myself down. We talked for a while staying on the floor, since I refused categorically to sit on the bed or on the chair. After one hour, I started feeling better and decided to get on the bed slowly. In that moment, I remembered our first night and what she told me about her ex-boyfriend who convinced her that sexually she was a cold woman. I watched her in the eyes and said, 'Get naked in five seconds.'

She looked at me, connected my words in the brain, and turned herself suddenly with a body torsion. I had my head facing the wall since I was binding my hair before the battle and I couldn't see what she was doing, but I could guess by the floats of dresses and underwear flying in the air and on the floor that she was actually getting naked. I took her in my hands and I demonstrated her that she wasn't frigid at all, as probably all the people in her block could declare, bringing in front of a jury audible proof. I asked her how she felt since finally she could be sexually satisfied, and she told me an Italian sentence I said once when she was particularly sexy with a short skirt: 'Complimenti a mamma,' meaning 'I have to congratulate with your mum for your beauty.'

From that day, the English students I knew who already considered me as a monster able to make people cry at will, attributed me the power to get people naked within five precise seconds. That night she confessed me how much she had been devastated by that detached and scornful 'OK...' I had e-mailed her. I promised her I wouldn't have left in that way anymore. I wouldn't have left her anymore in any case. After a couple of seconds though, I realized that my attitude would have brought me surely to act in that way again and how much that promise was worthy a penny. So I told her, 'I can't promise you that I will never leave your room anymore, but I can tell you that even if I might go away, I'll always go back to you at some point.'

Soon after I could see how much I had influenced her mind and marked her culture, corrupting her education. She was taught to remain always dressed, and of course, this applied also for sleeping. After one week in which I had been sleeping every night naked on her bed, as my usual way, she let herself go another time. I was about to fall asleep when suddenly she looked at me, she watched herself and her Indonesian dress, she faced me once more noticing that I wasn't feeling ashamed for my nakedness, and finally she took her cloth off with only one gesture of freedom. Her body, just like our first night together, didn't stay exposed for long, since my shadow didn't wait for covering her completely, glad of that re-found bodily freedom. She wouldn't have been able to sleep dressed in my presence anymore, as she perceived the pureness of nudity between people falling in love with each other. Yes, because one week later, I would have grasped her between my arms in the darkness of the night, and told her shameless that I loved her. It was the first time I said to a girl, 'Ti amo.' Usually, I left my love to be eaten by the crows throughout the long silences of unrequited love, so when staying with girls, it wasn't for love, since those girls I loved were always away from my destiny. Hanging out every day together, our disinterested way of staying together turned into something stronger. I thought she already loved me from that first brave e-mail she sent me, and so confessing her my love was for me nothing but unifying our common feelings, but actually, she wasn't in love with me yet. The night when I told her, 'Ti amo,' I had mistaken her silence for shyness. She just hugged me for long time, leaving me breathless.

One night she had a terrible cough attack. I brought her on the bed, taking her right from the floor where she had fallen. I rolled up her blanket and I looked after her all night long, without falling asleep. I used to change on her forehead a rag drenched with warm water every time it was becoming cold and dried. I didn't do it because I felt "obliged" as a compulsory duty of the boyfriend or because I wanted to be kind with her – I've always hated guys acting in a sweet way with their girls – I would have done it with any other person in my "club" of valuable friends. Actually, it wasn't even for goodness, I never considered myself as a good person. It was the pure will of act, just like when I kept on moving the snails away from the road, helping them to reach the green grass of the woods, when I was wandering around the forest of Toscana on my own at 16. I was afraid they would have been smashed by some stupid walking man or by a car or a farmer. That night, I don't know why, I just did it. After that night, some time passed by before she told me that I didn't have any idea of how much she was in love with me. I didn't act in that way for making her love me, but actually that thing unleashed her feeling for me. No one ever treated her in that way or looked after her – except her ex-boyfriend that time. Her father wasn't kind to her at all. That's why maybe... I looked after her that night for instinct, because my dad always looked after me when I was sick when I was a child, ignoring his job or if he had to take my mum somewhere. So it was a way of acting that I learnt naturally. I felt a bit sad when it wasn't for shyness but because she wasn't still in love with me that night when I had confessed her my love, or maybe she was already feeling something but she was unaware of it. I was astonished to learn how such a simple gesture for me had such a great power. It was the first time in my life that I loved and I was loved.

The Trent's Clock

'What's the time for God's sake? What's the time? Two minutes to midnight! I shouldn't have put these leather shoes on! I cannot even run! Such a stupid pain!'
I run from the station till the taxi area. To make things worse the driver let me off at the wrong campus' entrance. It was too late, I knew it, but I wanted to try anyway. That damned clock on the Trent building wasn't even showing me the time. Every time I was looking at it was always hidden by a tree covering the sight. Six square meters of clock totally useless. Out of breath and with a fewer shoe – one shoe less – I reached her Hall and checked at her window. What did she say?
'I'll keep the light on till midnight then I'll turn it off and go to sleep. While the light is on I'll wait for you.'
I have been living with Gigì for almost five months and things were totally fine, although we were perfectly conscious that very soon she would have left along with the coming of the first February snow. I wasn't too sad though because I was distilling every second spent with her, facing fearless the imminent departure as pending and peremptory. It would have happened in any case, so the best was to enjoy it. I don't regret those quick days, since every night was magical and one of a kind. She used to make me laugh with her clumsy ways – more than once she fell off the chair shouting as a child with windy hair – and her behaviors almost com-

ing from a cartoon with all those systematized expressions depending on the situation. I asked her once for pure curiosity why she never made up, and she replied me that she was too lazy for those long processes. In short, she should have woken up earlier if she wanted to make up, but she was a sleepyhead after all. The day afterward I met her in the morning while I was going to my lectures, a couple of hours after our morning separation: it seemed ages. She looked at me and said, 'Don't you see anything?'

I watched her carefully...I didn't get it. Then, while smiling at me, she batted her eyelashes repeatedly as her eyes were two butterflies mad for love.

'Ah! You made up! I'm sorry, I was checking the dress, not your face.'

From then, every time we were on the bed, I always asked her to do again that kind of batting, because it gave me always a strange intimate and funny feeling, especially when I closed my eyes and it seemed to me to be truly in a fairy and butterflies Kingdom. I found out later that she used that batting for implying dirty terms which because of her education and shyness she didn't want to say. We started to share even the rest of the day, without leaving our passion just for the night, when we used to lock each other in our perfect and less concerned world. One night there had been another damned Formal, ceremonious dinner where you have to dress smart, held every two months more or less, when in theory they serve decent food, although it's never sure. I've always hated them as just other public events marked by social rituals. I could see the people's hypocrisy getting busy for trying to be all friends and pretending to get on very well with everyone, even just for one night, although maybe they had been bitching around each other all year. What was to be celebrated then? Nine thousands pounds per year just for your courses or the fact that for once you could eat in a decent way? – for the English standards of course. I've always hated Formals since my first year. When Sandra looked at me and smiling said, 'Come on please, smile and be happy!' I couldn't hold the situation anymore and I ran away leaving the food as I found it. I had no doubts of where to go: Gigì would have been there, waiting for me. When I went to her room I was a bit drunk because for calming myself down, I drank some bottles of wine while the Formal's slaughter was carrying on, full of fit girls not even if it was a casino. As soon as I got inside her room dressed as I was, she spotted suddenly that I was quite tipsy. The fact that she had never seen me in a suit was making her very benevolent in love, and while she was taking my blue shirt off with elegant and firm gestures, she confessed me, 'My ex-boyfriend used to drink quite often, and I didn't like that.'

'Oh well, I don't drink that much, so don't worry.'

'No, but I like you with that whimsical behavior and the alcoholic breath.'

With a satisfied yet compassionate tone I declared smiling, 'Your ex is such a poor guy though…if he drank, you didn't like it, but if I do it, you do. If he cried, you considered him as a weak person while if I cry, I'm fascinating to you. You don't like people who smoke, but I can bet that if I ever smoked, you'd like it.'

'It's just that you're different from other people...'

That unrestrained run toward her room turned me sad and depressed just thinking that when she would have left the UK, I wouldn't have anyone to run to during those kind of situations when not even John or Freddy could understand me. She always kept the light on, and so every time I left my Hall, I would have walked confident that at some point not far away I would have seen a shining light, with a girl always checking diligently at the window, waiting for me. 'There it is!' I thought every night. I used to whistle and as soon as she spotted me watching her from the road, suddenly she would have run downstairs for opening the block's door, with her Indonesian dress which every time I had fun with lifting it while doing the steps, making her laugh of embarrassment while I pinched her legs running away from my fingers. Sometimes she came over in my room cleaning it or trying to make order in that mess, but the more she tried the more she understood the IMPOSSIBLE of doing it. So she used to make me laugh every time for the way she was blaming me pointing with her forefinger at that mess. My usual move was to take her fingers in my hands, starting to suck that innocent finger, convincing her to forgive me, but turning into a bigger mess my room with our love passion. That was a happy period I will never forget. Probably the happiest months of my life where everything was perfect, no frustration, pain, despair, problems. I knew that in a case or in another, she would have been there, at the window, waiting for me.

Nonetheless, I was still ignoring one thing. I was still a child on this point of view, because I hadn't experienced yet a terrible concept. She brought me to learn though. One night it was already late, at least 11.00 pm. She asked me if I wanted to hang out for eating Chinese noodles. I refused of course, because I wasn't hungry, because I didn't want some Chinese food, because I was tired and wanted to sleep. That rejection though, caused in her a typical female reaction: the day afterward she started to test me checking the situation, proposing me all those things she had never obliged me to do before, only to understand if she had the control or not, trying to impose me to agree to do things I didn't want to. I was realizing what actually she was doing. I only thought it was a period where things were going like this. Everything blew up one night when I told her, 'Listen, you seem my mother when she annoys my father duly every Sunday or holiday for doing something of special, funny, or in any case, out of the routine. Every damned New Year's celebration she always wants to hang out going to the cinema while we – my dad, my dog and I – obviously don't want to. Every time she makes typical female scenes because she's too spoiled and if she cannot obtain what she wants she annoys my father till death for one year, till he agrees reluctantly. He must have a liver full of bile. I don't want to become like him, and for sure, I have never thought you would ever be like her!'

'So one day, if I want to ask you to eat out or to go to the cinema together, you wouldn't please me, would you?'

'Of course, I wouldn't if I don't want to. I want to feel free to do what I really want to, respecting you, of course.'

The conversation's tone started to become strangely serious. I wasn't understanding: everything started from a simple invitation for eating out. She was disappointed, and started speaking harshly, 'This is a big problem...because not now, but maybe within some months I could get tired of you if this situation doesn't change. Now it's still acceptable, but as time passes, my requests could become more important, dealing with more serious topics, and your rejections would count a lot because you do not want to make compromises.'

At this point we were sat on the bed, facing each other. The image of my mum and her figure weren't separated anymore, they were more than just specular, they were the same: I could see her annoying me on Sunday for going somewhere I don't want to go, while I just want to sleep or to make love. To make things worse, I kept on having an image in front of me, appearing and fading away. All my life I've spent as long as possible in the forest, close to my house on the hills, sitting on tree's roots, and reading, and looking for myself in the shadows of the forest. That green and intense image kept on visiting my eyes, fading more and more. No more green boughs. My heart was bleeding in rivers of black death. That memory of freedom was getting cancelled, threatened by compromise. I didn't even know what a compromise was! I've never even used this word in all my life, nor I had heard about it. I hadn't studied it at school nor I had read books talking about it. What was she saying? What was that term implying? Did it mean going to eat noodles in the night? I didn't have any clue, I only knew that it was a concept I didn't like. She was becoming just another teenager willing to make me feel a puppet. Why did she want to ruin everything between us? Only to have a proof of my love? I was totally gone. I was only sure about one thing: my eyes were full of hate as she could see it herself, clearly and without any misunderstandings. She wasn't scared though, but she had a tiny bittern smile with sad eyes, conscious of my limits toward a relationship and knowing that it would have been all ended that night, because of her will of control. She was keeping her look down, without being able to stand my hateful eyes for long. I was breathing quite heavenly, with my eyes out of my face. I couldn't hold that situation anymore and I got up, I needed some water. I had absolutely to calm myself down, otherwise I would have turned upside down her stupid room within four seconds and a half. While I went to get a glass of water, I noticed that she left her head going down, dejected and hopeless, as someone offering the head to an executioner. There was no need to ask me if I wanted to leave her or not, I think my answer was obvious. After that look that I gave her for ten minutes without talking, I couldn't watch her anymore. Since she spotted me ordering my things, I told her, 'Don't worry, I won't leave now,' making her understand that I wouldn't have gone away from her room in the night once again, like when I made her cry the first time, although it was clear that once I would have left in the morning, I wouldn't have returned anymore. I'm not keen of promises. I lied on her bed. She didn't even dare to touch me. She knew me after all. I tried to sleep but I couldn't. I have been staying awake all night long. At some point, while she was sleeping, I went to sit down on the armchair at the feet of the bed. It was dark. I was watching her sleeping thinking about how much funny was her unconsciousness toward what was happing in her room, toward the fact that she couldn't even image the rage inside me while she was dreaming. I was scared of myself actually, thinking of my figure half-hidden in the dark, cold and detached. In those shadows surrounding me, I was alone. Truly, I didn't know what I would have done: if before I was sure that I would have left her, now I was starting to think and think and I couldn't find any solution. I was reaching the conclusion that only when you live alone, you can avoid making compromises with others, and also that every relation imposes compromises to be accepted, nullifying your Ego, bringing to a voluntary frustration. 'This is the prize of love: yourself,' I was thinking. At this point she woke up slowly and noticed that I wasn't next to her anymore when her hand, wondering around the bed, didn't find my body asleep underneath the cover sheets. She started fidgeting in a clumsy way. She wasn't among those morning people able to wake up quickly. Her head was lolling around in silent complains. Probably she thought I have already left. Actually, it wasn't an option I excluded. She started checking around the room with her weak eyes, and surprisingly she noticed my coat was still there, hang on the door. I was feeling almost pleased by that show: not only because I could see what would have happened if I had left, but because she was giving me the pride to be among those people who as soon as awake, they can do everything quite quickly. She seemed to me like a quarry I could have easily hunted in that black forest in which her room was turned. I became pure shadow. Scanning pitifully the room, she lingered on the armchair on which I was sat. I was feeling inside that kind of excitement as I were playing hide and seek. She sighed deeply when she finally saw me, distinguishing my figure from the armchair, understanding that it wasn't a Chinese ghost hunting her from Shanghai, but it was her pissed off guy. She gave me her hand, lying on the bed still half-asleep. Painful for having woken up, she whispered, 'Please, come to bed...'

    I didn't act too much in a reluctant way because I really needed to go to bed. I laid down next to her. I turned her so she would have given me her back, and I hugged her in that position. I didn't know what to do, nor how to do whatever I wanted to do. I realized that if I still wanted to keep that warm body clung to me, there would have been only one thing to say, 'I've decided one thing.'

    'This is our last night together, isn't it?'

'Starting today... I will eat as many noodles as you want,' and I held her ardently to me, crossing the borderline between childhood and maturity.

It wasn't the pain I felt for love to make me change as I thought, it just made me become more conscious and disenchanted. Actually, after many meditations, I understood that that two things mainly distinguish a child from an adult: patience and the ability to make compromises. Her imminent reaction sweetened what for me had been an important but bittern decision. I felt her body trembling and trembling, crying sobbing and I couldn't get why. Then finally, she turned to me full of tears with the most honest smile I had ever seen. By the way, those noodles we went to eat some day afterward sucked and watching me in pain for what I was tasting – actually I was about to throw up – she told me that I wouldn't have had to eat anymore noodles for her. Laughing, I told her to fuck off.

After having reinforced our bounds and made our relationship more mature, without illusions, happened a very dangerous working chance. Uncle Toni, the Roman, wrote me that since he was in London, he wanted to arrange a dinner with me and the Spanish woman as well who happened to have a house on the way to Nottingham, in a God-forgotten village on the Trent. He told me that the Spanish lady would have been very glad to host this dinner in her house, and actually she was already cooking the paellas. I trembled a little bit because I knew it was a good working chance, since it was important for me to keep connections with these kind of people and maybe arranging future projects, but I also knew that she would have tried to make a move, and maybe I would have succumbed under her sexual appeal. After all, only by thinking about her I used to be turned on like a pork. The Spanish woman used to write me short but quite clear e-mails, about the fact that she was still thinking about us. I used to reply her with the same tone till I stopped writing her in a romantic way since I met Gigì. In general, I was confining the conversation on compositional problems about my new scores. I've always said everything to Gigì, and of course she knew about my Spanish affair, and she was even jealous about it – as you can imagine – because of the way I used to decant the qualities of a mature woman and our wild sex night. She knew me after all: I'm frank and merciless. Till the last moment I didn't know whether to accept the invitation or not. Then at the end, it was Gigì that convinced me to accept, saying she trusted me, underlining also the importance of that dinner for me. Poor her...poor me as well because from that dinner I wasn't able to arrange a concert, not even a small performance. The Spanish wrote me her address and we agreed that I would have brought her some new scores I had written for violin. At least it wouldn't have been the two of us at dinner, but Toni and his wife would have joined us. My journey to go there was quite desperate, because since I had little money, I arranged the whole travel with busses and coaches to reach that abandoned village. I arrived toward the sun setting, after almost 3 hours and a half of journey – by train, it would have taken me 35 minutes, but, who had the money for it? I kept on thinking about how much the UK is so well organized in terms of coaches and busses that are able to reach every place throughout England with a small fee. In Italy, you need a miracle to find a coach if you want to get to a small village or isolated town, and even harder is to find a box office. They're always late and drive really badly. I don't know how many times I had been throwing up on those monsters when I was a child. Coaches are like trains in the UK, and they're also fucked comfortable, like a first class ticket on the plane. Maybe because they know trains are really too expensive and they are even unhandy. Travelling to that village really fascinated me, because I had the chance to contemplate the spectral mist typical of English Gothic sights, romantic at the same time. It seemed to me that my bus, on which there was just me, the driver, and a very awkward man with two little dogs, would have been ambushed very soon by a wolf man waiting for the right moment. The gloomy trees that prevented me from having a clear prospect of the road, were terrifying me. In the meantime, I was repeating what Gigì and I said before my departure, thinking about the dinner, 'I'll wait you till midnight, then I'll turn the lights off and I'll go to bed.'

'Let me see...my train should arrive around 11.40 pm in Nottingham. I hope I'll be able to get in time to the campus. At most, we can see each other tomorrow...'

'Don't make me get worried...'

Gigì - An Italian in Nottingham

I reached the village – it wasn't a village – with the illusion that I would have found her address quite easily. I didn't. Truly, her street belonged to the newest part of the town, almost in periphery, and so when I started asking around for indications, no one had any clue. I started getting worried when even the postman didn't recognize the address. It was cold, very cold. I like traveling painting crude maps on a piece of paper, but sometimes ignoring the real measures and distances fucks you over. In a sense, I like travelling in a random way for testing society, for checking how many people are willing to help a wanderer. I like inspiring compassion to people. I adore making them feel good people, proving their merits. It's a sort of social experiment and every time there are bad, good, lazy or useless people. Finally, a young guy declared to know where that place was. He was talking with a quiet difficult accent for me, and all I understood was that I had to find a pub called "The Crazy Monkey" quite far away. I started walking. I asked for indications in pubs, whose names are impossible to find in Italy like "The veins of the digger", "The King's Hammer", "The Glassy Oak", "The Cat's Piss", "The Pot after the Rainbow", "The Spit of the Gipsy", only for quoting the most interesting ones. It seemed as everyone knew about this pub, this "Crazy Monkey", and I was starting to be excited by the idea of finding it, if I would have ever found it. Finally, I reached it; it was nothing but a kind of depot on a car park with this big wooden monkey as signboard. I went there asking for indications since by then there were just few yards separating me from that damned address and I was starting smelling the paellas. It was 6 pm and the pub was already full of drunk people. Two women shouted at me when I got in, telling me to fuck off. I ignored them because many times when some friends of mine replied to insults in pubs, it ended up in a fight with knives shining in the dark. The owner pointed me out the right way I could already see under my very nose from the pub. I went to check it over, and I heard the noise of plates someone was preparing on the table. I walked around 8-9 miles from the place the bus left me to the "Spanish house". I changed dresses in the street, no one was there anyway. I knew I would have walked for a long time, so I had brought the shirt with everything else needed for an elegant dinner in a bag. I couldn't hope to do 10 Km wondering in the mist demanding my clothes to be still presentable for a dinner. I took the jumper off and I put it on an iron stake with the rest of my stuff. I was half naked in front of her house. I don't even dare thinking what she would have done if she ever knew it. Facing my strip show, there was a big house where a big party was on. I even had the idea to squish in looking for a toilet where to get changed, since I often used to get changed in public toilets before important meetings. It always made me laugh thinking that apparently I was presenting myself in a perfect and elegant way at dinners with ambassadors, meetings with journalists and critics, concerts, conferences, and every time without letting transpiring the fact that few minutes before probably

I got changed in an open air garden or public toilet... even in winter. Every time I went to London by coach for work, I always got changed without problems in the pub in front of the coach station – without problems is a way of saying, since the bog was one meter wide and one and half long. When I rang, I realized soon that I had arrived too early and that probably I wouldn't have found anyone. If I hadn't had Gigì, there would have been time for a quickie. She opened the door and I saw her for the first time after three months. She had an obscene dress, quite tight and purple, underlining the lines of an over forty woman who doesn't go for running every day for sure. I liked her curves, but not when emphasized in such a bovine way, strangling almost the whole body. We started talking quite formally: I was longing to tell her once for all that the situation had changed, but I didn't want to. I don't know why, simply I didn't mean to. One thing I did though, was to make clear that my last train for Nottingham would have left at 11.00 pm, in order to make her understand that I would not have stayed over there for the night, as I would have done if I hadn't had Gigì. I found myself repeating the train issue many times throughout that night, as I wanted to convince myself or remind myself not to stay and fuck her after dinner. She was about to ask me if I had found a girl worthy of my music, when thanks God, Toni and his wife arrived. We started eating smoked salmon with butter and caviar that Tony had just bought fresh in London for 400 pounds. It was a little can, pretty like a marble. I adored Toni's twists.

Then we started eating paellas, but I was already too tipsy for appreciating it. At some point I played on the piano of the Spanish woman my last concert for violin that I had hoped to perform soon but I never did it. Everyone was so surprised and astonished when I confessed that I had been walking from the bus station that one month later when I had to meet Toni and his wife in London, she wrote me begging me to avoid walking from the station but to go straightforward to their house first, closer to the station. They would have been in charge to bring me to the concert we had to go to: 'Please, please, don't walk!' I like when people know my particular behaviors and extravagances, underlining them in a positive or negative way, asking me to avoid them. The time to say goodbye arrived sooner than I thought, giving me the chance to say once again, 'At 11.00 pm I got the train for Nottingham.' Toni acted in a very gentle way and avoided having me walking back again, since he offered me a lift to reach just in time the last train which was already leaving the station. The Spanish woman couldn't hide a bit of disappointment for the lonely night waiting for her, but after all, Gigì was waiting for me.

I was running so desperately when I finally reached the campus because I wanted to prove to her that she didn't have any reason to get worried, and also that I can distinguish between career and sex. I didn't want her to go to bed without knowing that I loved her even if we would have seen each other the day afterward. I was caring so much about running to her, and let her kiss me with thousands of caresses that I didn't even give a shit wrecked my shirt during the run, and of having lost one leather shoe sink in the Trent's mud, while taking what I thought was a short-cut. 'Keep it if you want! And if you wish, I can throw you the other one, you stinky son of a bitch!' More than the *Lady of the Lake*! The Trent was a bully with a knife that I had learnt to treat firmly, a scum who had been spying all my movements since the first day with Bess. Finally, I reached her window. The light was still on. With the very last breath I had, I made a whistle that could have called even Cerberus from the Acheron: 'If I do this last whistle with the last breath left in my lungs, at least I'll die conscious that Gigì will find me having heard our love signal.' I didn't die. On the contrary, I saw a long dark hair girl who really astonished run at the window and happy she hailed me that she would have come down quickly. 'Don't worry, I won't even move,' I thought, 'rather, maybe I'll lie down on the roadside.'

She reached me and with a love kiss, she gave me life again, or better, she gave me the strength to say a couple of disconnected words on the evening. The essence of what I had to say was already implicit in my act, as well as in my hot body after a run that could have been lasted for all a past life. I walked on the steps following her like in a sort of trance, and when I've arrived in our room, I jumped headlong like Goofy on the bed, with the only consciousness of loving and being loved.

Reale degli Antoni

May

When I saw the snow, I wished it could be November again, so that I could have cherished your soul and push your eyes down the Moon Valley once more, but the Gods don't fulfil the wishes of a poor lover. I'll be alone on the river this summer. Suddenly I'm afraid. I live just for seeing you again, you'll never lose me. Ti amo.

There was an Asian girl having breakfast in the Dining Hall that morning. It was Saturday. Her jumper with pandas on it was quite irritating me. Why did it have to be pandas? I had the feeling she was doing it on purpose: 'Well, if you're talking about pandas...' Why did she have to ruin my breakfast? I couldn't hold it anymore and I left. One of the first Chinese terms Gigì taught me was how to say bamboo. After hundreds of efforts for remembering the correct word, I asked her, 'Why the hell will I have to use the word bamboo?'

Trying to justify her linguistic madness, she said, 'No, it's very useful...like if...if you're talking about pandaaa," and I laughed for the kindness she pronounced that word. I hugged her.

Gigì had already left some months before, and I've found myself wandering around the valley's shadows looking for reasons to stay alive. My Dantesque journey was leading me every time to the window where I used to whistle every night, waiting for her to appear and run to me. Strangely though, the room hadn't been occupied by another student yet, and the window was always dark. I thought it was a good thing since I didn't want someone else to occupy what had been "our room". Some day before she left, I had promised her to be faithful. It was worthy. She asked me, 'Why don't you come in Shanghai to visit me… If you betray me then don't come.'

She was right. We went too far from the mere physical experience for deceiving us that we could have kept this relationship on a superficial level. We had to take it in an extreme way: we could have left each other or we could have sworn each other's love, trying to hold the time and the distance separating us. In fact, in theory I mean, I would have gone to China in September to visit her, meaning that I would have seen her again after six months. And so I've promised her to be faithful and that I would have loved only her. Actually I was loving only her, the Moon and my dog. After some weeks from her departure though, I was trying to analyze my life, my situation, and it seemed to me that I was trying to find whatever and however excuses for betraying her. The days were endless, although I kept on trying to focus on my courses. I was thinking, 'I would say that I need to live my life, considering Gigì and me as in a sort of long term relationship. I'm seeing her again in September, and I have to be conscious of this, but it's not fair that I'm forsaking the best years of my life for a girl I met only four months ago. So any sexual experience I would have had with another girl, it would be wrong to define as betraying, since there's no relationship I would corrupt. That's a good thought.' As you know, the campus wasn't the right environment for having these kind of thoughts, since betraying – or not betraying, this was up to the way I would have considered it – wouldn't have been difficult. There were a lot of girls I liked, something I wasn't forgetting to report to my Gigì when I wrote her. The point was that I would have never found the courage to betray her, and that was it. I couldn't ignore the pain I felt every night for the distance separating me from my love. Going to bed was the hardest time, I was missing her so much that I literally couldn't breathe. I had never passed through something like that. Then in the night I used to wake up and ask myself surprised, 'Where's Gigì? Where?' without finding any consolation. Replying to me, she was saying that she didn't want me to be so upset and desperate, she was urging me to love her not so much. What a fucked sentence! If I had loved her less, I would have never accepted a distance relationship, and what a distance! I would have never thought to remain faithful with all the fit girls living in the campus and surely I would have spared my heart from nightly extreme pains.

If you remember, I mentioned that I founded a sort of fight club among the internationals of my Hall. Well, this began to be a very pleasant hobby, beating people up in the free time. Maybe those documentaries on lions influenced me too much. I was always scared that the Dean would have found us out soon or later, but luckily he had never spotted us since he was too busy looking for the guys who had ruined part of the Hall with a fire extinguisher, after having destroyed all the cameras. Alessandro, the other Italian attending the club, had the ability to make me cast doubts on my love. He was teasing me since he couldn't understand my faithfulness which he defined as stupidity. He had two relationships simultaneously, one in Parma where he was studying, and the other one in Rome, where sometimes he had to go for visiting his parents. Nonetheless, he succeeded in cheating on the already deceived girls, with another one, but just for one-night-stand, nothing serious. He was telling me that I was wrong to take life and especially my relationship in such an extreme and fair way. He used to argue on the importance of living in the present, getting laid with every girl having big boobs. He didn't care that much about the face, as far as the girl had nice tits. One day we went to a pub, he and I, and suddenly he noticed that there was a table with girls being about 18-19 years, looking at us constantly with great interest, probably they understood that we were Italians. Even if they kept on watching us in a very *anti-sgamo* way all night, we both knew that they would have never made the first step. He was similar to me on this aspect: if he understood that a girl could have liked him, he would have gone to talk to her confidently. The only problem was that he didn't know UK as I did, he didn't know that girls, unless drunk, wouldn't have been honest toward their passion. We waited for them to get out the pub for chatting them up and then he approached one of them asking for a lighter. We started introducing and talking, but after a few seconds, we understood that there would have been no hope for us and we left.

'Why? Why for fuck sake?' he was asking me. 'Why if you keep on watching me for all night long as you were interested in me, when finally I make the first step for making things easier you almost ignore me with a fucked snob attitude?'

Poor Alessandro. I had already gone through this. Laughing, I had to tell him a lot of stories about this and the first months of my English experience, starting with a girl whose hair was like copper.

Maybe he was right talking in that way and trying to convince me to live my life, I don't know. I just knew that if there was nothing bad in sleeping with someone else, I wouldn't have felt any sense of guilt. While if I felt physically bad only thinking about it, it meant there was something wrong. Betraying would have been wrong and the trick for avoiding a tragedy was to reject every situation potentially dangerous, without being cast into a series of events impossible to avoid once started.

I nearly died one night. While I was having my usual evening walk around the valley, looking for valuable points for betraying and finding reasons for feeling guilty, I saw Gigì's room illuminated after more than three months. I couldn't resist going and checking who was there, so I walked toward that block. I didn't do it only for curiosity, I guess I did it also for a sort of dominant instinct that pushed me to reclaim my domain, the place where our love was tenderly sleeping, as I wanted to defend it from unknown intromissions. I had been waiting out of the block for someone to get out of it when finally a guy arrived and kept the door for me. I walked the steps quite hastily, possessed by a kind of mysterious inner force urging me to run and run as if the demon of my madness was chasing after me. I was living again physically those moments, making the same steps of the same block in which Gigì and I had been meeting every night. Reaching the top I stopped myself suddenly: the door. Her door. On the stair there was the same smell felt when I used to undertake it with her. The same warm air coming from the radiator close to the bathroom. Everything was just like I remembered. This is what I couldn't explain to my heart. This is what he couldn't understand. 'If everything was the same, why she wasn't there?' A bit for all the stairs I made running like a mad person, a bit for all these thoughts that I had, I laid down on the wooden handscroll, focusing still on her room at the end of the corridor. After a while I gained strength again and I started walking slowly toward the door, step by step. I had to grasp all the courage still remaining in me for knocking and preparing for the consequences of what I would have seen. Maybe Gigì would have welcomed me and I would have found out that this was just a nightmare. Maybe a beautiful girl would have opened the door and I could have stayed in that room with her all night long telling her my sad story. Who the hell would have been there? While I was waiting for someone to open it for me, it came to my mind the moment in which we said, 'Goodbye.' That day she bought a wooden postcard in a small shop in the city-center, and after having written her Chinese address on it, she said, 'Send it after I leave. Write something nice on it please,' a postcard that I sent with the first February snow full of romantic bullshits.

We spent our last day packing up and preparing her baggage, bringing some objects not fitting into the bag to some friends of her. She couldn't believe that I really wanted to keep them, but I insisted to have our cover sheets and the big tiger who would have stayed with me throughout all those months. It was gigantic. Nonetheless, in May when I came back to Italy, I succeeded to convince the flying assistants that I would have been able to stay for the whole flight hugging the tiger who didn't fit into my bag. 'If we fall, it's going to be my airbag,' I said whimsically.

Since I didn't have any pillow, I kept one of her as well. She was so spoiled. Unluckily, we didn't enjoy our very last hours because we might have a problem: she had a delay on her period of ten days. So we started asking ourselves what would have happened, making plans for an option or for another while we were waiting the time when she would have had to go. At 4.00 pm she would have taken the train to London, starting her long way back to her home, on the other side of the world. I was quite worried for the situation and my hair was becoming white because of the stress, although after one week we found out that it was nothing but a very strange delay. She wrote me the good news from China on Saturday morning, the best day of my life, if you know what I mean. Suddenly it was 4 pm. She didn't want me to take her to the station and so we said, 'Goodbye,' on my room's door, in the corridor at the top floor of my corridor. I leaned an arm on the door, vertically, stretching my figure, watching her as saying, 'There's nothing we can do.' She was watching the floor. At some point, since I was perceiving a lack of pathos during those last moments, I told her, 'Can you play the piano? Ehy,' lifting her chin toward my face, 'Can you play the piano?'

Her eyes started becoming wet and out of the blue, without even being able to hold her one last time, she run away, stopping herself only at the middle of the steps looking at me. Maybe she stopped because I called her, but I'm not sure if I actually did it.

'Bye bye,' she said, trying to smile and holding her tears, as all the words I said about being faithful and going to China wouldn't have been true. It seemed that it would have been the last time I would have seen her.

'Ciao.'

She ran away while I was holding myself, it would have been worst to reach her although that violent detachment wrecked me in many pieces. Every morning when I was leaving her room, I used to put my shoes on sat on the bed, while she was having fun in tickling me with her feet, pretending to be still asleep. When I was leaving her block, I was singing every time.

Here a very English girl opened the door: an OK blond who seemed to me boring and faking her seriousness. As soon as she opened the door she watched me thinking, 'I guess you got the wrong room.' While I was talking to her, I was exploiting every moment for looking behind her shoulders and hurting me: everything was different inside. On the shelves where Gigì used to keep colorful and happy candies, there were some sort of grey medicines. The armchair was moved and all the odours were totally different. Well, what did I expect?

'Oh, I'm sorry. I think this is the wrong address.'

'Yes, I think so... Who were you looking for?'

Right in that moment I didn't know what to say, but then I found unreality and the impossible a better and truer answer than others. I said, 'I was looking for a Chinese girl.'

Still today it makes me wonder a lot her unconsciousness. The point is that I was actually looking for my Chinese girl over there. The absurd of that conversation and her irresponsible arrogance while trying to look for something vaguely logic from that meeting. She would never have understood what that sentence meant to me: looking into the impossible an absurd truth for deceiving my heart unable to understand the reality of things. It still obsesses me her ignorance about what happened in that room, the words and the oaths made, the screams of ecstasy and the deep breaths, the beauty and the truth of that little world which till that moment had been MY reality.

'I guess downstairs there are some Asian girls...

maybe you can ask them.'

'Yes, I agree. Just asking but, when did you move here?'

'A couple of months ago.'

And I left. Strange, although she had moved over there long ago, I had never seen the light at the window on. I left, it's a way of saying: even if I already knew the way things were, that check really shocked me. It's like when I used to try to make my dog understand that the park wasn't opened at 6.00 am, and when we used to arrive and find the gate shut, she watched me, 'It's not my fault,' I used to tell her on the way back, trying to justify myself in front of her beautiful green eyes.

As soon as I got out of the block, I didn't know where to go, I just wanted to avoid meeting everyone and everything reminding me of her, so basically I needed to escape from the whole campus. While walking around, I found a green place a bit isolated where I hid. I climbed on the highest tree and in that dark paradise of forgotten dreams I could find a bit of rest. In the shadow at least, I wouldn't have been able to see my torments walking in front of me like a group of whores with confused skirts. I remained there, on that tree for a while, watching from a distance some students walking without spotting me of course, as I were already dead. I was staying there, remembering Gigì's passion for my hateful eyes, when she used to wander around on the shores of the lake with me, studying the reflections of the light that dancing on the lake, reached the veins of my dark eyes. She was amused by them, as my eyes weren't common ones.

To make things even more complicated, toward March, Gigì started telling me that she might not have the strength to resist for many other months, and that she wanted absolutely to come to Italy as soon as possible, probably in April or May, without waiting for my coming in September. But she would have never come, because for doing it, she should have told her parents about our relationship, who wouldn't have taken it very well. She was the only daughter they had, and surely they wouldn't have agreed in "giving" her to a stranger who in their view, would have taken her away from them. They would have considered me as a sort of threat. I heard many times these kind of stories while talking with my Chinese friends. It made me think a lot when I heard that the parents of a guy from Shanghai were against the relationship he had with another Chinese girl only because she was two years older than him. I could say that this was an attitude strictly belonging to Chinese people, whose mind was ancient and closed, but I must confess that also in Italy things like this were happening – a friend of mine had been contrasted by his own parents only for having thought to have a relationship with a girl without a planned career. So as you can see, it was more to be analyzed case by case, although in Asia parents intromissions were more often and extreme. Since my parents have always left me free to do what I wanted, I couldn't understand nor tolerate the parental authority when it has to do with private feelings. In short, why cannot they think about their own business? However, the problem persisted since she wouldn't have told her parents for the fear of the consequences on her life and on our relationship, and so, she wouldn't have been able to come over to Italy to visit me. For me, it didn't represent a big problem because by then, I got already used to the idea of seeing her only when September would have come, but she kept on pressing the matter, having this absurd idea of coming to Italy in May. How? One day of early April when we were video-calling, she told me about her home situation, a condition in which I had passed through as well. I won't try to explain you the tragedy that all these events had on our relationship, since she was afraid of being betrayed or even to be able to betray, following the destiny hunting her family for generations. Right when she was starting to cry for fear of the future, that damned laptop stopped working, leaving only the audio on. And so I found myself listening to someone crying without even having an idea if she could hear me or not. Trying to understand the different sounds I could get from a desperate video-call, I got the sentence, 'Maybe it's better if we leave each other before something happens.'

Worried about what was happening, I started a very cool long speech which saved my ass another time. I told her, 'I will never betray you because I keep on weeping since you left and girls cannot be attracted by me in this way,' trying to cheer things up a bit, 'But if you will ever betray me, don't worry, because it would be only my fault, because I wouldn't have loved you enough. It wouldn't be your fault because if my love couldn't prevent this, it would only mean that I wasn't loving you with all my heart.'

She would have never betrayed me because she cared too much about me, in fact I believe that she just needed to conceive a relationship without guilt or negative roles, without feeling condemned to something unforgettable, and moreover, girls never tire of hearing the words 'Ti amo'. With my rhetoric skills, along with a non-working laptop, speaking with someone who might not even have heard what I said, having my back fucking hurting, I succeeded in fixing up a situation full of bullshit, since nothing of serious had happened and where only smoky thoughts were remaining the real threats, problems without any consequences. When I finished speaking I didn't even have a proper idea of what I had said but soon after that long speech, the laptop started working again and the image that I was looking at was the one of a girl completely at peace, with a seraphic smile. She wasn't talking. She was staying there, watching me, making me understand that my speech worked quite well. It calmed both of us down. To be fair, even the idea of her father in that moment wasn't annoying me, besides, if I had seen him, I would have even kissed him. I was happy because in the total panic, I had found a quite logical thought that cast us into another realm. I was sat on the floor, propping with the hands behind, looking at her with a hallucinated site. I was in love with the whole world for the first time, and I didn't even know why. Maybe the key was that I had conceived a reality without faults nor delicti on our emotions, where people could love honestly and be frank among each other. Now I was embracing all the people of the same world I had hated and disgraced without any resentment. And this was beautiful. She was watching me on her behalf with an ecstatic smile, and said, 'What you said is so nice... I feel that finally I have found the courage to tell my parents about us.'

'Are you sure? Well, I know that things are going well between us but once you told them you cannot take it back... I'm afraid of the consequences you would have to face. I don't think your parents would give you the permission to come to Italy to visit your guy. I don't think it's a good idea. I'm worried although right now I'm at peace with the world and I cannot think about anything bad.'

'Don't worry, now go to bed and tomorrow when you'll wake up, I'll have good news.'

Index

Reale degli Antoni

PART ONE: An Italian in Nottingham

An Italian in Nottingham	7
Cheese and Wine...a lot of wine	19
Perversions and Possessions	31
The anvil	41
My murdered friend	53

PART TWO: Gigì

A good academic start	61
Kansas City move	85
Gigì	109
The Trent's Clock	125
May	143

www.ingramcontent.com/pod-product-compliance
Lightning Source LLC
Chambersburg PA
CBHW021439080526
44588CB00009B/595